SOFT FRUIT GROWING

FOR THE AMATEUR

WHAT TO PLANT, HOW TO PRUNE AND MANURE, WITH A
CHAPTER ON NUTS, ONE ON MUSHROOMS AND
ANOTHER ON COMPOSTING

BY

RAYMOND BUSH

ILLUSTRATED BY THE AUTHOR

First published as a Penguin Special, December 1942
Revised Edition 1944
Second Revised Edition 1945
Third Revised Edition 1948

ISBN-13 978-1-4067-9354-3

CONTENTS

FOREWORD

BEFORE even thinking of an introduction I would like to say that I have had so much help from so many people—especially in additions and corrections for the second edition—that I hardly feel justified in describing myself as more than part author. I do not believe that there is any profession in the world which is so generous in the exchange of information as the fruit-growing fraternity, and take this opportunity of saying so. The fact that this revised edition contains flat contradictions of a few statements made in the earlier editions should not be held against me. The fruit grower must be prepared at all times to alter his opinions at short notice. To be useful a handbook should be revised every year.

February, 1945.

The only addition I have to make to this Foreword is to thank kindly readers for further hints and suggestions, many of which I have incorporated in this third edition. In response to many requests I have also added a chapter on Mushroom Growing.

December, 1947.

Revisions for this 1948 edition include the chapters on Raspberries and Strawberries. Next time I shall have to re-write the lot.

RAYMOND BUSH.

INTRODUCTION

UNDER the pressure of post-war restrictions horticulture has "gone to it" with a vengeance. Peace in Europe has been achieved, but restrictions remain. All over the country gardens continue to be rescued from the insidious advance of the artichoke patch and other less useful weeds; battalions of plum suckers are being uprooted and virgin meadow land, complete with wireworms, is being well and truly dug in order to comply with the aerial advice of our Mr. Streeter

As with the vegetables so with the fruit, and where there was no fruit it seems that a multitude of fruit trees and bushes are now being planted by the amateur—nothing else can account for the extreme shortage of stock and the corresponding high prices ruling to-day.

Starved of fruit-juices and their pleasant vitamins, with the heavenly aroma of black-currant pie but a memory of the past, the raspberries and strawberries gone with the cream, it is small wonder that the old Adam is arising in his might determined to grow more fruit and enjoy it.

Fruit can be grown almost anywhere if you are prepared to take the trouble. There are frost-proof and almost fool-proof sites where fruit seems to grow itself and there are very, very difficult sites, but from any average soil a good return may be expected, It would, however, be a perfectly simple matter to plant trees or bushes or canes or plants of various fruits using poor strains of those fruits which would never be profitable in any soil. This is a point which most books on fruit growing omit to mention. Not only is it vital that the stock be sound but whenever and wherever fruit is planted, since it is destined to remain there a few seasons or many years, preparation for planting should be as adequate as possible.

Because of the longevity of many fruits it is a wicked shame that really close inspection of nursery stock for sale to the public is not enforced. Admittedly it consorts well with our own disregard of racial improvement and our slip-shod pure food legislation, but it is not right that an investigation in 1922 should show that raspberry varieties were inextricably mixed and that one variety masquerading under a dozen different names was being freely distributed and planted out all over the country. Equally damaging has been the planting

out of reverted black currant bushes, apparently strong and
healthy but physically incapable of ever carrying a crop of
currants. Strawberries, also, infected with virus troubles
and doomed to collapse before ever a fruit was picked. These
are examples from the dark side, fortunately incidental and
not general, for research and improvement in our fruits
goes on.

In every decade new varieties of fruits are introduced by
their optimistic progenitors. Heralded as the best ever,
tested and proved to be so or found wanting and discarded,
their life may be long or extremely short. Occasionally a
newcomer makes an instant hit and remains a fixed favourite
and a household word. Such are Royal Sovereign and Sir
Joseph Paxton among strawberries and, of more recent introduction, Lloyd George among raspberries and Laxton's
Superb among apples. For every one that survives a hundred
perish and are forgotten, and it is a strange thing that many a
nursery catalogue still lists varieties which are but shadows
from the limbo of the lost.

Yet, however excellent a variety may be nothing but the
most painstaking efforts can keep it so. Growers and research
workers to-day are combining to rebuild and fortify these
valuable strains of fruit. We have seen the insidious reduction
in strength of strain in Royal Sovereign, in many areas Sir
Joseph Paxton cannot be grown at all, Lloyd George raspberries are dwindling in stature all over the country. Our apples
are made of sterner stuff, as are our pears, but microscopic
infections can and do invade our plums and cherries.

The commercial grower, I think, suffers far more than the
amateur from large scale troubles. His policy of spraying
hundreds of gallons of wash on every acre of his fruit in
order to kill his enemies must be sufficiently drastic to wipe
out many of his insect friends. Nature's balance is upset and
a happy medium is missed. The growers' manurial programme
also is altered since the change over from horses to tractor
means that a few drops of spent oil now lie where once the lordly
muck-heap breathed fertility. Again Nature's balance suffers,
since the cheap manures which he buys are not always those of
natural organic origin but are often merely synthetic substitutes
lacking those "trace elements" whose importance is even now
scarcely realised, and which, unless used wisely, spell
unbalanced growth and lowered resistance to the attacks of
insects and disease.

Markets for the commercial grower change with the moods of industrialism or the advances of scientific discovery. Slump in the coal-mining industry depresses the plum trade. The discovery that pectin, which is needed to set certain jams, can be more cheaply extracted from apples than supplied by gooseberry juice, brings down the acreage of berries in the Wisbech area by hundreds. Cold storage too, by bringing the world's fruit to our door, has altered the whole set up of English fruit–growing in the past fifty years.

The amateur fruit grower is spared all these things. He is not restricted to commercial productive varieties of fruits but can concentrate on high quality rather than mere quantity. Raising fruit for his family, his sole concern is supply. The demand is always there. Not for him the grape thinnings from Worthing masquerading as choice young gooseberries, the sloppy strawberries from the coster's barrow or the half-filled punnet of sodden raspberries; he sups with Lucullus and lives on the best.

Dealing as he does with a small patch of ground he can do it well. Does a black currant bush revert he can pull it up and replant from his own little nursery (provided that he can detect reversion and knows how to strike a cutting). He can build up his special strain of strawberries, rooting out any that show signs of trouble, limiting the runners from his best plants and providing himself with new plants to succeed his old ones. Where small-scale fruit growing is practised each tree can be—so to speak—manicured to a perfection which is impossible to most commercial growers. Early years should be experimental. It is well to be inquisitive and the art of looking over fences may be both enlightening and productive. Fruits have definite likes and dislikes where locality is concerned.

Even to the amateur the manure problem is bothersome, but where farmyard manure is out of the question almost identical results can be had from compositing house and garden refuse, for the analyses of the two show little difference, and small additions of organic manures such as meat and bone meal, hoof and horn, shoddy, dried blood and so forth will supply all that he is likely to need, save where potash is obviously required.

Having got so far, many a would-be gardener will say here "What about spraying? I suppose he'll expect me to do hat." Well, although there do seem to be a few blessed spots where greenfly cease from troubling and weevils are at rest; where fruit has achieved some marvellous balance of its own, such places are very few and very, very far between. Too often the amateur is satisfied with his crop because he does not know what a crop can be. Spraying can be a preventive of trouble as well as a cure, and there is no need to wait till sawfly caterpillars have stripped your gooseberry bushes of fruit and leaf and are standing (as they will) on their hind legs craning their heads upwards in search of fresh leaves and goosegogs new. A dash of poison on the leaf before they hatch and the trouble will never arrive. So, it should be a source of solid satisfaction to be able to scotch a pest with a quart or two of the right remedy instead of waiting till gallons cannot bring back your lost crop. You will therefore forgive me if I do not let you off spraying.

Half the tedium of pest control is inability to realise what is taking place. The life histories of many pests are amazing. Believe me, under his microscope the research worker sees among these minute insects which plague us, happenings so enthralling and so incredible that to him the war between Man and the Insect is a very real struggle. Knowing even a little about your insect pests is a very great help in fruit growing.

I

AN OUNCE OF PRACTICE IS WORTH A TON OF THEORY

THERE are certain cardinal rules in good fruit growing which must be observed. They are:

1. If you are to have full control of your fruit it must be planted in separate rows or blocks and not interplanted with lettuces, rows of carrots, onions and so forth. Do not forget that I said full control; there are some who insist upon irises beneath their apples and geraniums between their gooseberries and heave a sigh to think what a lovely bean might be grown up each raspberry cane.

2. Most fruit is planted to remain in position for a long time (I know two apple trees that were planted over two hundred years ago and still crop heavily). For this reason do not grudge to any soil or site the preparation which may be necessary or advisable. You cannot crack up the subsoil after you have planted your tree, and if drainage is necessary it is easier, cheaper and better to see to it before you begin planting.

3. Certain soils suit certain crops. It is far better to grow a few suitable varieties well than to have a considerable but mainly useless collection of unusual specimens.

4. Fruit must never be crowded. Ample room to expand and to allow the entry of sun and air is imperative. There is a minimum distance to allow between each sort of fruit, but there is no maximum.

5. Having secured sound fruit trees or bushes and planted them well and truly (contrary to general opinion the particular phase of the moon does not matter) it is up to you to maintain them in a state of fertility and health. If neglected deterioration can be rapid and irremediable.

6. Descriptions in catalogues are not always accurate. Too often, where the raiser's own introductions are described, modesty takes a back seat and optimism is over-stressed. Nor are new varieties necessarily the best constitutioned or the heaviest croppers and where quality varies but little it is better to grow a heavy cropper than a smaller weight of bigger berries. Better a reliable old variety than a doubtful new one.

Let us take these six maxims and see what they involve.

Why Fruit Should be Kept Apart.

1. The up-to-date commercial grower has long since ceased to interplant his tree rows with vegetables. Such cropping is left to the market gardener whose fruit trees are a very secondary consideration. He has several reasons for not taking advantage of every inch of open space in order to grow more produce. Land rent is the lowest charge which he has to meet, therefore convenience and the reduction of labour costs is worth considering. The ability to cross-cultivate his crops with tractor-drawn tools is too great a blessing to dispense with. If he is constantly handicapped by rows of lettuce or greenstuff, he must use far more labour to keep his crops clean or be content to make a poor job of his culture. Not only that, but spraying is interfered with or entirely ruled out; indeed, if he wishes to winter wash his trees, there can be no autumn-planted cabbages for him, for the caustic wash will scorch them. Manuring interplanted crops does not always suit the permanent fruit trees or bushes. Green vegetables have different needs from fruit trees. The former may be longing for irrigation and nitrates to develop succulent sap to feed robust hearts while the latter need semi-drought and starvation to ripen up next summer's fruit buds.

If the size of the garden allows, each variety of fruit, be it apple, pear, plum, raspberry, gooseberry, currant or strawberry, should have its own allotted space. Only where space is important should interplanting be done and then under limitations which we shall discuss later.

Pre-Planting Preparations.

2. Since soils vary enormously one can hardly expect all gardens to offer equal facilities for fruit growing. The low-lying garden, sheltered though it may be from the wind and deep and rich though its soil may be, is from its very situation at the mercy of every spring and autumn frost, while the garden higher up, despite its shallower soil, gets the wind but escapes the frost. When the low-land gardener finds his dahlias and runner beans are black after the first October frost the high-land gardener's are green and happy. So if you are in a low spot expect some damage most years and a wipe-out occasionally.[1]

[1] Some idea of what fluctuations in crop may be caused by frost damage can be drawn from the figures (bottom of page 13) on a big commercial fruit farm part of which is situated in a very frosty site.

No English fruit that I know of, with the possible exception of the quince (which loves to have its toes in water) and the cranberry which prefers bogland, can abide water-logging, and good drainage is half the battle in fruit growing. The heavy soils are usually the ones which need drainage to free them from surplus water while the lighter soils have to be assisted by water-holding manures to retain enough. Come to think of it, the immense latitude in soil conditions, varying as they do from the heaviest weald clay to blowing sand, which fruit will tolerate is an astonishing fact, but in every gradation from clay to sand the tree roots must have enough soil and enough moisture if they are to flourish.

You will find fruit trees or bushes growing well on soils where the water table is within a foot or two of soil level, as in part of the Wisbech area and Lincolnshire, and you will find them thriving above 500 ft. up on the Hampshire greensand. This, however, is of little concern to the amateur who has few pretensions to geology or water divining and merely wants to grow a little fruit. For a test of his soil drainage all he need do is to dig a few holes in different parts of his garden to a depth of two feet. If during the winter months he will observe the rise and fall of water after rain, in these holes, and note if it drains away rapidly or stays put during the winter when evaporation is at its lowest, he will soon get some idea of whether his garden soil can be relied upon to attend to its own drainage or is in need of a little assistance.[1]

Granted that the garden does need drainage, how is one to set about it? Sometimes there is no fall and no available

[1] Stagnant and running water seem to affect trees differently. The cricket bat willow likes to be on the edge of a running stream but not in a swamp. For some years I watched a black currant bush growing and cropping quite happily rooted in the bed of a hillside stream. The temperature of the spring water may have been conducive to winter survival of its root system, but in any case one would not recommend planting in streams, quite apart from the nuisance of having to paddle every time one wanted to pick currants for a pudding.

	Bushels of Apples.		Plums.	
1935	Frost	600	None.	
1936	Glut	45,000	12,000	baskets
1937	Rest	18,000	9,000	,,
1938	Frost	12,000	410	,,
1939	Glut	59,500	6,000	,,

outlet for surplus water such as a roadside ditch. In such a
case the land would be liable to flooding and so would be
unsuitable for fruit. Although it is possible to make soil
mounds and plant apple trees atop of them the system would
hardly be feasible for soft fruits. Where there is enough
fall to lower levels and an ultimate outlet there is a choice of
a variety of methods. Our grandfathers laid blackthorn
branches at the bottom of their drainage trenches and then
filled them in. Some of these thorn drains can still be found,
though they have long ceased to function. Clinkers or stones
can be laid in trenches, as can anything else which will prevent
the soil from sinking back and compressing itself once more
into an impermeable mass through which water cannot
percolate easily. Land drains or tile drains laid at 24 ins. to
20 ins. deep in a sort of herring-bone formation are the arable
farmer's and pukka fruit grower's solution of the problem
and these are obviously the most efficient if the most expensive.

On lands which do not hold up water in the trial holes
further drainage is unnecessary, but deep cultivation, which
means breaking-up without bringing-up the subsoil, will help
any type of heavy soil to free itself of surplus water and will,
in the case of light soils which tend to dry out, enable the
gardener to work in water-holding humus in the shape of
compost or farmyard manure. We shall hear more of compost
later.

Especially intractable soils can at times be vastly improved
by firing small charges of explosive, well underground, where
the trees are to be planted. This must be done by the expert,
but there must be many available now that the sappers are back
home again. The breaking up of the subsoil favours wide and
rapid root action, and I recall a site at Hitchin where two
plum trees planted on a site where two Zeppelin bombs fell in
the last war very soon grew away from their companion
trees.

The gardener's ideal soil is a warm, deep loam overlying
chalk. He does not often realise that ideal, but when he does,
and appreciates it, results can be superb. Far from ideal is a
stiff, shallow clay liberally besprinkled with large flints with
chalk beneath. One finds much of this type of soil on the
high lands of Bucks. To cultivate this soil is no job for a
woman, for it is sticky in winter and adamant in summer. Light
soil on chalk is not at first sight encouraging but provided
the energy is there to dig out sizeable holes, removing the chalk

and replacing with fertile top soil, some surprising results can be had. On a Surrey hillside where some 6 ins. of light soil overlaid the chalk I found that while some three-foot was the stature of a sweet-pea plant grown *au naturel*, by excavating to 3 ft. deep and filling up the holes with soil a 10-ft. plant was quite easily obtained.

This may seem a great deal of trouble to go to, but since a tree will often outlive its planter, what is an extra quarter of an hour when putting in a fruit tree? We have not mentioned sands. As a rule only the richest are ideal for fruit, but they are so easily worked and can be enriched with a minimum of trouble that good results can usually be obtained. The coarse sands and the gravelly lands are the poorest, being usually deficient in humus and short of potash and phosphates, and very liable to dry out in hot weather.

Suiting the Crop to the Soil.

3. You can of course suit the soil to the crop, but this is apt to be expensive and takes time, unless you can invest in truckloads of loam, cubic yards of sand and are able to corrupt the local dairyman's morals to such an extent that he will betray his farming and part with his manure. To begin with then, if age allows you time, plant moderately and experimentally, and base future planting (and once you have begun nothing but lack of space will hold you back) on results. You may think I am stressing the point when I advise you to suit your crop to your soil, but here is a case in point. The apple Warner's King used to be a very popular sort, but it was always extremely liable to canker, and for this reason went out of commercial planting, but one particular grower of my acquaintance found that this apple on his particular soil simply could not go wrong, and whenever in doubt as to what to plant in went a block of Warner's King. If such examples interest you, here is another. Those two well-known varieties James Grieve and Blenheim Orange are usually able to grow well enough on clays, loams and sands, but in the happy days before the present war when fruit growers used— around Derby Day—to meet in force and tour the orchards of England, I recall visiting a big farm on the east coast where, although most apples did well enough, it was simply impossible to grow these two. They reached a certain age and then, like the young ladies of the Victorian era, went into a decline.

It is because of suitable soil conditions that so much of Cambridgeshire went into gooseberries, Norfolk into black-currants, Essex into Cox's Orange Pippins, and the Blairgowrie district in Scotland into raspberries. Because of soil and earliness the Southampton area has become famous for straw-berries and because of its chalk and ragstone Kent has become the cherry producing county. So I think you will agree there is a good deal to be said for first suiting your crop to your soil and then seeing what can be done later to perfect the soil for the crop.

Elbowroom in the Fruit Garden.

4. If you want healthy fruit space is very important. Sun-light is the prime mover in the chemical process of growth. Air and water are equally vital (Plate I). With these essentials, plus food, the leaf chemistry of the tree works at full capacity, food stuffs for bud and blossom are compounded, wood growths complete their ripening, and a constitution is developed which makes invasion by fungus troubles unlikely.

If you wish to have large, well grown gooseberry bushes and fine black currant bushes you must allow them the full space to develop in. Better a row of four at 6 ft. apart than a row of six at 4 ft. apart, although, as we shall see in the case of the black currant, which is thornless, certain liberties may be taken.

There can be no denying the fact that the previous generation of nurserymen were responsble for the overcrowding of commercial orchards. Their aim, naturally enough, was to sell as many trees as possible, and because of this their recom-mendation was always to plant everything too close. A grower who planted apple trees on stocks of moderate strength was always advised to plant at 12 ft. apart. With the young tree this space at planting time looks absurdly wide; ten or fifteen years after, when his trees were in full bearing, the grower found that they had filled the space to such an extent that cultivation and spraying was becoming impossible. Also, being deprived of full light and air, instead of growing out his trees had grown up in a vain effort to avoid each others shadow. So he is compelled to pull out and burn alternate rows, thus altering his plant to 18 ft. A few years later he will find this close enough and there is no doubt in my own mind that an 18 ft. plant in the first place would in the long run have given him better trees and more fruit.

You would fancy from this that commercial growers would not make such errors twice, but I regret to confess that, having some nice fruit bushes available, I tried to crowd more into a given space in my garden than I would advise anyone else doing, and as a result my wife will have to pick currants on all fours or I shall have to remove alternate bushes, for there is no room to get between them.[1] Close planting is really a form of cruelty, and but for the fact that fruit trees are not vocal more would be heard of it. Only if you can be firm about early removal of alternate trees is close planting justifiable.

What's Bred in the Bone.

5. Stamina, breed, background, pedigree—call it what you will—should always be looked for in selecting trees and fruit bushes for the garden. A scraggy, starved specimen may eventually be induced to grow into a moderate, or even a fair, specimen, but it will seldom equal the best.

I knew a twenty acre patch of Victoria plums which was "wished" on a grower who knew little of fruit. He knows more to-day. They were throw-outs, with thin, crooked stems, and worked on the wrong stock. They never grew and prospered. Bacterial disease invaded their stems, killing them off in tens and twenties yearly. They never cropped, for there was no wood to carry fruit, and the last I heard of them was that three quarters were to be pulled up and the best used to gap up the quarter that remained.

There used to be a strain of strawberries growing on the north side of the Malvern Hills, high up and away from all risk of infection. They prospered exceedingly. Year after year they cropped, the berries grew to a magnificent size with little manuring, and local growers knew that when these berries, which were a little later than theirs owing to elevation, came on the market, they must be prepared to sit back and take second place. Plants lasted seven or eight years, but I doubt they are all gone now. Some years ago I managed to get some of them for a friend and advised that they should be grown alone, since Royal Sovereign is self-fertile. But no— the friend wanted Tardive de Leopold, a big strawberry but not of the same quality, to interplant. The Tardive runners were obtained and planted, and all died the next year or

[1] Since this was first written a season has passed and I have removed alternate trees. They are now 8 ft. apart and at this spacing should do nicely.

became hopelessly involved with virus disease which they brought with them. The Sovereigns, after another year, began to go down with the same trouble and a good strain was thus wilfully thrown away. Incidentally the Tardive plants cost just three times as much as the Sovereigns.

The importance of strain is realised by our Research Stations when testing cropping powers and response to manuring. It is useless for them to take half a dozen strains from different sources and expect similar results. A strain must be chosen and enough plants must be raised from that strain, or even a few individual plants which show particular promise, before a worth-while trial can be started. That is why East Malling Research Station in Kent, which is particularly concerned with strawberries, offers its members plants from its own selected strain which they have found to be very good.

From these examples it will be realised how important strain is. It can be a fugitive asset if neglected. One must rogue one's strawberry bed, one's raspberry rows and one's black currant patch for undesirable abnormalities, getting rid of them at once, otherwise the particular virtues of the strain may be lost.

A Rose by any Other Name.

6. You will, of course, have noticed how superlative in quality all fruits are—in the catalogue. If a pear can possibly be considered edible it will be described as "luscious, melting and of superlative flavour." Having grown it you may well decide that it is hard, gritty and altogether beastly. When an apple simply cannot be described as good for dessert or even cooking the scribe will bite his pen and indite it as 'Very large and fertile. Fine for exhibition." A plum which even the plum-sawfly maggot will jib at may well be written off as "the ideal dual purpose plum," taking great care to specify no particular purpose.

Well, they have their excuses. We grow pears in England and some—Williams and Conference and Comice—are excellent pears, but we cannot grow superb pears by the score of varieties as do the French unless we put them against walls and so donate them that bit of extra warmth and comfort which compensates them for the lack of a European summer.

Commercially, very few varieties of any fruit are worth growing, because the public has become accustomed to a few varieties in the shops. These varieties have been grown in large quantities because of certain inherent qualities such as bright colour, good keeping and toughness to stand travelling. Also fruits must be relied upon to provide continuity of supply over a definite period, thus allowing the retailer to stabilise his sales.

If you are no fruit grower, consider for a moment what fruits you know by name, let alone recognise when you see them. In apples, Bramley's Seedling, a big green cooker and possibly a Codlin? In dessert apples Cox's Orange Pippin and Worcester Pearmain? No more. Can you tell a Lloyd George raspberry from a Pyne's Royal? How about cherries? Morello you probably know, and also a Whiteheart, but can you tell a Royal Sovereign strawberry from a Paxton or an Oberschlesien? I find the above 'quiz' is a fair average, and when one considers that there are about 2,000 named varieties of apple, and hundreds of plums and cherries, it is readily realised how hopelessly dependent upon description the adventurous beginner must be.

In making your selection you can be sure of one thing, and that is that the commercial grower of to-day plants a variety because he is sure that under normal climatic conditions he can rely upon it to crop regularly. An old and trusted survivor is bound to have merit. It may not be the merit you are looking for—that remains to be seen—and meantime new sorts may be increasing in popularity and justly so, but unless you have money to burn it is a mistake to pay high prices for a few new varieties on the basis of an enthusiastic description. Pioneering is always expensive.

So, in this chapter, we have explored six points, I hope with profit, for, if not, yours will have to be the hard way of trial and error with no short cut to the Garden of Eden. Having said which we will now get down to practice and leave the theory alone for a little.

II

COMING DOWN TO EARTH

ONLY the few can aspire to a walled garden, which in these hard times is perhaps just as well, for, single-handed, one can scarcely hope to keep up with the work. Wall-fruit is a specialised type of gardening which demands head-gardeners and under-gardeners. The head gardener of one of the stately homes of England told me a few years ago that where he once had seventy men and lads in the gardens he must now make do with two landgirls and a boy. It is a subject on which expensive books are published, and, as such, has no place in our considerations. In so far as the garden wall of the small house is concerned that shall be duly discussed, but our main consideration at the moment must be the fruit side of the amateur's kitchen garden.

Making the Best of Your Soil and Site.

Since you cannot easily alter the position of your house and garden you must make the best of what you have got in the way of soil and site. If you were choosing a site for a new house and garden you might, with advantage, call in an expert who would examine the structure of your soil and subsoil, boring into it with an outsize in augers and bringing up a soil pattern lodged in the twists of it; or he would order you to dig a hole 2 ft. or 3 ft. deep so that he could examine the soil structure from the cut side of the hole and thus assess likely possibilities and estimate the need, if any, for drainage.

By persistence and politeness it is possible to get the advice of the local County Horticultural Adviser, who is paid out of the rates. He can arrange a test for definite acidity (lack of lime) or of the essential elements.

This is "de luxe" selection and outside our province, so, disregarding your particular sample of soil, look around and see what the condition of the various trees, and even of the weeds, may be. Trees, by their growth, will show depth of soil and possibilities of root penetration as well as water table, if it be near the surface. Weeds will indicate by their particular varieties whether the soil is acid, neutral or limey.

It is a fruit-grower's maxim that land which will grow fine

elms, old hawthorns—particularly old hawthorns—and tall nettles, will grow good fruit. Elms must have deep rooting undamaged by water logging (I have traced a root from an elm through 126 ft. of chalk on the side of a cement quarry in its search for water and an old gardener of mine won many gallons of beer in the "local" by exhibiting a parsnip, which, growing through the side of a well, dropped a root 24 ft. to water and enabled him to take on all comers with the certainty of winning his bet). Nex ttime you travel through the midlands towards the industrial areas, where water-logged meadows are general, note the dead tops to timber trees and the stunting of growth on the low-lying levels. This is due to root suffocation, indicating that the main root system has reached the water level too soon or that its roots are drowned by winter rise of the water table. Yet, on the higher lands, you will see fine elms and oaks flourishing. As for hawthorn, it is one of the same family as the apple, and our grandfathers used the thorn as a stock on which to graft their apples with some success, so that old hawthorn may safely be taken as a sign of fruit longevity. Nettles grow best where humus can form rapidly, making a rich and friable top soil in which its roots can run. In itself the nettle is the best and most valuable of all humus-producing weeds which rejoice the heart of the composter, so that in these three we have all that we need to assure us that we can grow fruit.

Shelter.

It is pleasant to have shelter, especially against the North and East, and also against the prevailing wind, which is usually South-west, but which is, in any case, indicated by the green on the side of trees where wet has caused moss to collect. It is generally agreed that when one has a sizeable hedge or shelter belt the protection given extends 10 ft. for every foot of height. This means that within a triangle bounded by a line drawn from the top of the shelter belt of a 10-ft. high hedge to 100 ft. away at soil level an area of protection is given. Walls do not give this protection since they can cause eddies and back draughts, but they protect fruits which are grown against the walls. It will be noticed that a North wind blowing against a wall running East to West will cause leaves to pile up at the foot of the South side of the wall.

Trees and hedges slow down wind by filtration. The screening of hop-gardens by the use of a coarse net is a fine example of this slowing down of the wind. On one side of the net a gale may be blowing but on the leeward side only a gentle breeze. The leaf of beech hedges makes an almost complete barrier against wind, while the leaves of a belt of ash trees merely float horizontally in the gale while reducing it but little. Incidentally, it is this variation in response which causes the beech leaf to bruise and brown up when assailed by out-of-season gales which leave the ash leaf undamaged.

Shelter is best when associated with a slope which allows free air drainage from the site. If the land falls to an open aspect at its lowest level, well and good; shelter all round is not needed. As for the best types of tree for shelter belts and hedges near the fruit garden, evergreen trees are the most suitable, as these do not harbour the pests of fruit trees. It is a fact that certain pines are host plants for a fungus which attacks the black currant leaf, but the damage is not important. Hawthorn and beech hedges not only harbour fruit pests through the winter but, in the case of the former, provide and suffer from similar pests.

In the case of young gooseberry and red currant bushes planted in really exposed places shelter can be very effective in preventing strong young growths from blowing out. Black currants can suffer severely in a gale, and those of the last ten days of May 1942 completely stripped the crop in fully exposed situations on high land near the South coast. During the flowering season shelter is needed by the beneficial insects and, with the possible exception of the bumble bees which are the best friends the fruit grower can have since they are busy in all weathers from dawn to dark, many pollenising bees can only do their work effectively where they are not buffeted by strong winds. The hive bee, in particular, refuses to work unless the temperature is well over 50° F. and will double her work where sheltered flying is possible. In a bad season, when wet weather coincides with blossoming, every bee-minute is valuable and may make all the difference between a crop and a failure.

Frost and Fruit.

We will go into the subject of frost in its broader aspects later on, but, in the meantime, in so far as your garden is above the level of the surrounding countryside, be it on Streatham Hill or high up on the Chilterns, so will your risk of spring frost damage be reduced. We may say briefly that great lakes and ponds of chilled air collect in low places as heavier cold air drains off the upper levels and slopes. The depth of these icy lakes can vary from a few feet to hundreds of feet according to the contours of the district concerned. If you do happen to be in one of the low places you can reduce your risk of frost damage to some extent by planting varieties of fruit known to be frost-resistant, either owing to lateness of blooming or the particular make-up of the blossom, which, by its lightness and low water content, is less vulnerable to low temperatures than its more heavily-charged relations. You can also, by covering over certain fruits so that they are sheltered from what is known as "direct radiation loss," reduce the severity of the frost by several degrees.

Frost is a big and an interesting subject, but direct radiation loss operates in the same way—but in reverse—as does the variation in temperature between the heat of sunlight and the coolness of shade. Just as a cloud passing over the sun will reduce temperature for the time being, so will a cloud (or any other covering) raise temperature by reflecting back a part of the warmth being radiated away from the earth's surface on a frosty spring night.

Quality of Soil.

There are all sorts of interesting soil possibilities to be seen on a large-scale geological map of any district, and of late years comprehensive soil surveys of the fruit-growing areas of England have been published which make interesting reading for the serious student of fruit growing. Looking at these maps one sees how closely allied are rainfall and soils in providing the localisation and specialised production of fruit in the Eastern, South Eastern and West Midland counties. Small outcrops and strips of such valued soils as the Upper Greensand give Newick and Chailey, in Sussex, almost a monopoly in those enormous, yellow, Leveller gooseberries, while in Essex the warm brick earths and gravels, and the county's low rainfall, have made large-scale planting of Cox's Orange Pippins inevitable. In vegetable growing the naturally high potash content of the Vale of Evesham soil was appreciated by the monks of Pershore Abbey who started the industry in those parts. From the geological map one can trace out the rich stretch of famous fruit-growing land in Kent, warm loam on chalk, sweeping across the county from East to West in a ten mile wide strip from the coast to north of Maidstone and petering out at Guildford in the West. Equally important are the greensand areas. But we must leave the large scale and get back to our small particular site.

Preparation for Planting.

If the existing garden already contains fruit trees or, better still, if it is bare of any but there are fruit trees in the neighbouring gardens, many useful indications may be observed by looking over the fence (having preferably made the acquaintance of your neighbour first). Raspberries may be seen to flourish generally, gooseberries and currants may make fine bushes, or plums, pears and apples grow away well. Even trees and bushes which have fallen into decay may, by their stature, still bear signs of a vigour that was once theirs and which can be re-embodied by planting afresh.

From such indications one can visualise the possible capacities of the fruit garden. Let us suppose that the space at our disposal is 48 ft. wide and 60 ft. long. How best can we put it out to fruit?

We are a nation of bird lovers and many people would sacrifice their fruit rather than put an end to so jolly a companion as a blue-tit or a chaffinch. For these the fruit cage of small-meshed wire-netting is an expensive necessity. As wire is still almost unobtainable I mention the necessity but do not propose to enlarge upon it.

Planning the Lay-out.

It is a good plan to outline on squared paper the area which you intend to plant. We have chosen a piece 48 ft. by 60 ft. for our fruit garden. If you divide this parallelogram into 6 ft. sections you then have eight squares each of 6 ft. by 6 ft. Allowing a 12 ft. square for an apple, pear or plum tree, on dwarfing stock (i.e. grafted on to a stock which will restrict growth while encouraging free fruiting at an early age) you will have enough room to set out twenty of these permanent trees, one to each block of four six ft. squares, and you may also interplant between the permanent trees, for you will have ample time to take fruit from your bushes before any overcrowding begins; indeed, if your choice of permanent tree varieties is confined to thrifty growers and the most dwarfing type of stock is used, the soft fruit will be able to remain where it is for most of its profitable life.

In interplanting certain points have to be considered and observed; for example, if black currants are grown they are best used to interplant plums, since both like heavy nitrogenous manuring, while red currants and gooseberries are set among the pears and apples because phosphate and potash are more essential for all these on most average soils.

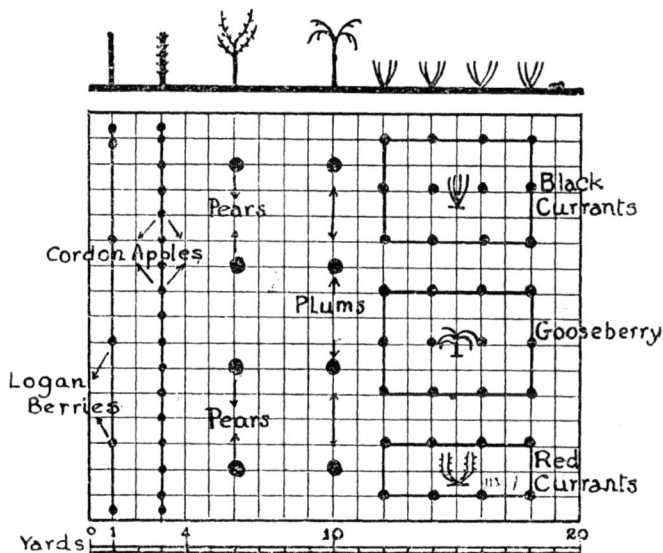

PLAN NO. 1.

How to use squared paper to plan out your fruit garden.   Each square is a square yard.

In plan No. 1, we have a fair selection of fruit: apples, pears, plums, red and black currants, gooseberries and loganberries.   Some people do not care for raspberries or logans, for all dentists are not as skilful as they might be, so if strawberries are preferred it is a simple matter to substitute four rows or so in place of them.

Plan No. 2 offers plenty of strawberries and raspberries and an adequate supply of red and black currants and gooseberries.   A row of berries, loganberries, black- or hybrid-berries is included and a number of dwarf pyramid apple trees or better

still pear trees which will always remain small and within easy
reach. Only certain varieties are suitable for this treatment.
Plan No. 3. Here we have cut out the strawberries—
there's no cream and not enough sugar anyway. We have
concentrated on cordon apples and pears while including the
usual soft fruits. Careful choice will be needed for the cordon
varieties. Plan No. 4 is mainly concerned with a straight-

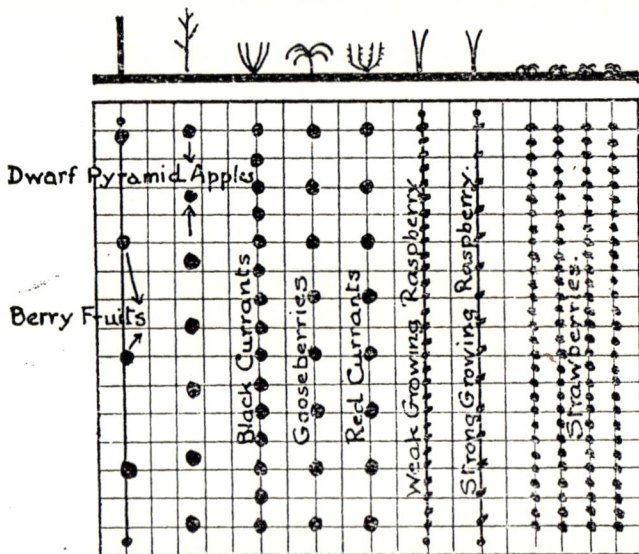

How to use squared paper to plan out your
fruit garden. Each square is a square yard

PLAN No. 2.

forward plant of half-standard apples or preferably bush apples,
with soft fruit beneath. A row of raspberries and two rows of
strawberries are also included. As the permanent apple plant
is at 12 ft. apart, thrifty growers on dwarfing stock will be
needed. In order to check growth it will be advisable to dig
up and root prune these apples about the fourth or fifth year
after planting. This will then allow a longer profitable life to
the soft fruits beneath.

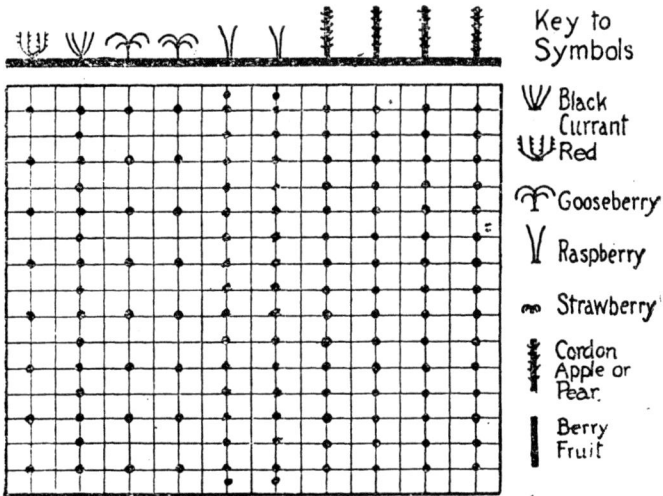

Key to Symbols

W Black Currant
UW Red

T Gooseberry

V Raspberry

∞ Strawberry

Cordon Apple or Pear.

Berry Fruit

PLAN No. 3.

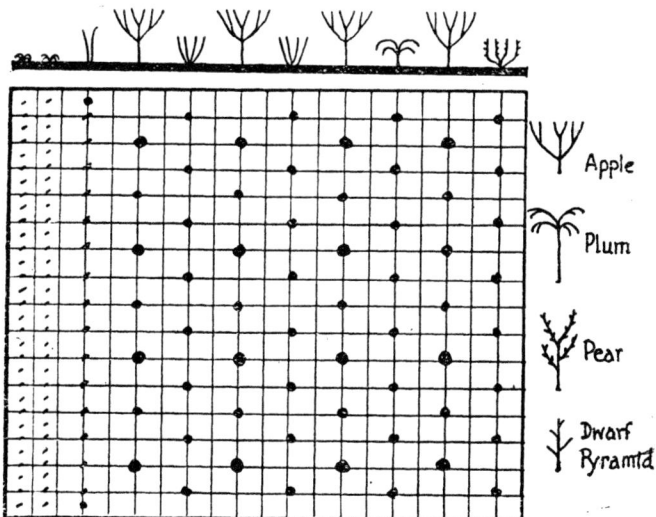

Apple

Plum

Pear

Dwarf Pyramid

PLAN No. 4.

The planting of cordon apples and pears means some outlay in posts and wire as well as more trees. The length of life of the cordon tree also necessitates something more permanent than a wood post. It is possible (when salvage officials cease from scrounging) to buy odd lengths of stout gas or water main piping. Eight-foot lengths, properly stayed and bedded into a block of concrete so that 6 ft. of pipe is out of the soil, will make an even more permanent investment than an Austin car. This type of fruit growing will be dealt with under apples. (*Tree Fruit Growing*, Vol. I.)

Dwarf Pyramid Trees.

This system of apple growing is popular to-day and in good hands can be very attractive. Astonishing crops can be grown and the trees are always well under control by spraying. Once the technique of pruning has been mastered good crops of apples can be expected with regularity. Pear dwarf pyramids are said to lend themselves even better to this form of pruning than apples and can equally well be included.

Close Planting excused.

It will be noted that in Nos 2 and 3 of these small-garden lay-outs black currants are planted at 3 ft. apart in the row instead of at 6 ft. apart as in the case of gooseberries. This is permissible because the black currant has no thorns and picking is simple. The same distance apart for gooseberries would make them almost impossible to pick since plenty of room to insinuate a hand is needed. Gooseberry thorns can be very poisonous to some people and are painful to everyone.

From these few suggestions all sorts of different combinations of fruit planting can be arrived at. The important point to remember when filling in the permanent trees of apple, pear and plum is to get the right varieties to suit the small space allotted to them. For example a Bramley's Seedling apple on a very dwarfing stock would fit in for some years on a 12-ft. plant, but one on the ordinary Paradise stock, such as Type 2, would need at least a 24-ft. plant eventually. A Lane's Prince Albert, on the other hand, even on a Type 2 stock would probably suit well enough for its lifetime. As with apples so with plums; a Yellow Egg Plum or a Victoria, worked on Egg Plum stock, would be satisfied with a 12-ft. plant, but a Belle du Louvain on any stock would outgrow it. These points will have to be considered when we tackle tree fruits, for very often the small garden is overwhelmed by some giant specimen which, while well enough in the field, is out of place in the small fruit orchard. If the amateur really wants to do the job well the best planting distance for a Bramley on Type IX would be 12 ft. to 15 ft. apart and on Type II a well-grown bush tree of twenty years of age will prefer 35 ft. to 40 ft. apart. These are commercial grower's figures and under the less favourable garden treatment the closer planting is suggested rather than recommended.

At planting time all the spaces suggested will appear absurdly large, and red currants at 6 ft. apart may seem wilful extravagance with the good earth, but, unless one knows one's currants intimately, it is wise to take no liberties with them, since extra space is always an asset, tending to help big growth and to donate quality and health.

The urge to include too many varieties is one to be resisted. In my time I have planted and tended "museums," have loved the beauty and deplored the quality or cropping powers of many a once famous variety. If I were asked to name what fruits I would recommend for the small garden I would give the following to choose from.

Strawberries.—Royal Sovereign, Huxley and Tardive de Leopold.

Raspberries.—Lloyd George and Newburgh.

Red Currants.—Laxton's No. 1 and Wilson's Longbunch.

Black Currants.—Seabrook's Black and Davison's Eight.

Gooseberries.—Whinham's Industry (red) and Careless (white).

Cordon Apples.—Dessert: James Grieve (1890), Egremont Russet (1880), Cox's Orange (1850), Laxton's Superb (1918). Cooking: Lane's Prince Albert (1857) and Edward VII (1908).

Cordon Pears.—Conference (1894), Williams (1770), and Durondeau (1811), Laxton's Superb (new).

Plums.—Victoria (1840), Yellow Egg Plum (1881), and Burbank's Giant Prune (1895).

As a matter of interest I have given dates of introduction in some cases, and you will note that there are very few new arrivals here. In the main they are old and trusted favourites giving good, regular crops of first class quality combined with moderate growth. Where the quality is not so good, as in the case of the plum Burbank's Giant Prune, and in the pear Durondeau, they are included because they have proved themselves able to crop and do well under almost any soil condition, which is no small asset.

Friends who know their fruits say that my list is far too conventional and that it is unfair to the nurseryman who is expected to keep going a huge number of varieties of great (though probably not commercial) quality. I quite agree with this view and am all in favour of those who have garden space planting a museum and adding to it annually.

Although in Plan 2 and 4 rows of Sovereign strawberries are allowed for they would be better elsewhere in the garden, since at even 6 ft. distance from the Lloyd George canes the row will soon be invaded by raspberry suckers and they are in any case likely to be overshadowed too early in the day. Where strawberries are concerned it is always preferable to treat them as a fruit divorced from the main fruit planting, since they can never be described as permanent and are not likely to enjoy a longer life than three or four fruiting years. Indeed the tendency to-day is to treat them as a plant to crop for one season only and maintain a planting sequence.

We can now put away the pencil and paper and turn to the serious business of visits to nurseries, which must be made if we are to get what we want—the best.

III

ON CHOOSING NURSERY STOCK

As apples and stone fruits are due for consideration in another book I do not propose to deal at all with these fruits in the short space available, and will therefore concentrate on soft fruits. The main idea of a small book must be to condense most of the salient facts into a compact space. For those with deep pockets who wish to know all about fruit I can recommend no better book than *Fruit Growing* by N. B. Bagenal, published at 21s. by Ward Lock & Co., Ltd., London. The author, with unlimited data, and facilities at his disposal, explores the whole subject most admirably and adequately.

A Little About Nurseries.

There are several types of nursery. Some concentrate on fruit trees, while others prefer flowering shrubs, dahlias and geraniums, but keep a little space for customers who insist on buying fruit trees. Some nurserymen grow trees and bushes "for the trade only" which means that, while they will supply the large commercial fruit grower and the town and country nurseryman, they will not do business with members of the general public requiring trees for their gardens. Others, of course, raise trees for all and sundry and what they do not grow they will "buy in." Fruit trees of all sorts may be "bought in" and "bedded out" in the nursery prior to distribution by the nurseryman. As one who has been a commercial grower I should be inclined to doubt the small nurseryman who stated that all he offers is his own growing. Some few can and do grow all they sell, exceedingly well, but the fact that a nurseryman "buys in" a portion of his stock does not mean that he cannot grow it himself, but that he has enough sense to go elsewhere for what he cannot equally well or economically raise on his own land.

It is a fact that the established local nurseryman can be very helpful in advising what varieties of fruit do well in his neighbourhood, and this should be borne in mind when deciding where to buy.

At times, looking over nurseries, I have wondered whether certain raisers of such things as gooseberry bushes, living as they do with their efforts always before them, do not suffer

from that same merciful parental complex which causes the
father to regard his very indifferent offspring as a miraculously
fine specimen.   For this particular fruit the war has brought
a demand which is amazing.   The gooseberry bush has taken
on the status of a gilt-edged security, and almost anything
which boasts a few stunted shoots and a vestige of live bud
is eagerly sought at fantastic prices.   In a few years' time with
fruit tree stocks more plentiful prices may go down but never
to pre-war levels.   We wish to avoid planting bad specimens,
and to make sure that we do not purchase rubbish we must be
able to recognise quality when we see it.

Taking our soft fruit groups alphabetically we start with
currants—black currants—and having once secured your
strain of currants the raising of fresh stock is so easy and
such fun that anyone can soon become expert and a miniature
nurseryman to one's friends.   At the end of 1939 my tennis
lawn housed 4,000 cuttings, and now in 1947 is planted to
raspberries.

Black Currants.

Black currants and red currants are two totally different
propositions both in habit of growth, pruning and manuring.
I have seen nurserymen grow black currants on a leg like a
red currant or gooseberry bush, but that is a very bad type to
buy.   The black currant bush when bought and when planted,
be it a one-year-old, two-year- or three-year-old, should have
a mat of fibrous roots from soil level to its extreme bottom.[1]
For a one-year-old good roots and a single, strong shoot
2 ft. to 2 ft. 6 ins. long, liberally studded at the base with pointed
buds, is all that is required.   After planting, the shoot will be
cut off and the buds energised into the production of new
shoots.   For a well-grown two-year-old four shoots are
usual and the strength of these will vary a little according to
the variety, Baldwin, for example, being a weaker type than
Boskoop Giant or Seabrook's Black.   While a three-year-old
is on the big side good results can be had, but for the amateur
two-year-old bushes are best.   Buy only "certified" bushes.
When buying currants and gooseberries buy early, plant at

[1] When a bush or tree has been dug up and has remained unplanted
over a period of days the bulk of the fibrous roots die.   Although
such roots may be described as useless to the newly-planted bush or
tree they are an indication of the virility needed to produce new
roots and as such are a valuable asset.

once and cut back hard. Then you can set out the various cuttings and have a nice little nursery of your own.

Red Currants.

In choosing red currant bushes it is better to start with a one- or two-year-old tree than with more mature specimens. Varieties differ a good deal in strength of growth in after life but this is less noticeable in their early years. A one-year-old will have two or three shoots, and a two-year-old five to eight. The latter figure will give enough main branches from which to build up a tree. If you are desirous of planting a row of Cordon red currants you may be able to secure bushes with only one or two shoots at a lower price. Since only one central (or two shoots in the case of a U cordon) shoot is needed there is no point in buying a well-furnished bush and cutting most of it away.

The root system of a red currant is far less fibrous than a black currant. When a cutting is made to strike as a red currant bush, the single length of shoot is stripped of all its lower buds leaving only three or four top buds which will be left above ground. Ths is done to prevent buds from below soil pushing up suckers; a very important matter in the case of the red currant, since the whole aim and object in fruiting this is to concentrate its energies into a very limited number of well matured shoots. In the case of the black currant we want as much new growth from below soil as possible, so all buds are left on the black currant cutting.

To make quite sure that the red currant does not make suckers it is quite usual to cut off roots from nursery stock which have sprung from the scars where buds were removed which happen to be near the surface level. This removal still further lengthens the bare stem of the red currant and one needs to be sure of plenty of root at the base of the bush, as for length of branch growth anything less than 10 ins. of young wood in a yearling or 12 ins. to 15 ins. in a two-year-old indicates a poor specimen.

Red currant shoots are brittle and break easily, so much so that in early years protection is needed against wind in order to allow the bush to grow enough old wood to shelter itself and develop into a shapely specimen. The shoots also are subject to invasion by the caterpillar of the Currant Clearwing Moth which, by tunnelling up the soft pithy centre, weakens the branch so that it will break easily if bent. Indeed, this method

B

of diagnosis is quite legitimate to determine the degree of infestation where the health of the young bushes is in doubt. If a branch breaks at a gentle bend and shows a blackened, hollow stem the nurseryman has no ground for complaint. Actually I have seen young bushes of both red and black currants so badly infested with this caterpillar that the constitution of the whole patch was weakened, for though growth continues breakage is frequent and unavoidable when picking and pruning and there is always a tendency for wood to die out.

Gooseberries.

Gooseberries are subject to amazing variation in quality. There are, of course, upright, strong growers and weak, drooping growers. These habits are incidental to varieties. The quality I refer to is constitutional. I illustrate three specimens drawn at random from different sources of supply. A yearling gooseberry bush can be simply a bit of stick with a few hairs of root at one end and an inch or two of shoot at the other, or it can consist of three or four stout, young growths (the season's growth is always very light in colour), springing from the wood of the original cutting and supported below soil by good, strong roots thrusting out from each bud scar. (In the gooseberry, as in the red currant, the lower buds are removed to prevent suckers arising from the cutting.) There may be three reasons for such variation. The cutting may have been a poor, unripened bit of wood to start with, it may have been good enough but taken too late in the season, or the nursery soil may have been quite unsuitable. Cuttings of soft fruits will always do best if they are taken as soon after leaf fall as possible and before the winter comes. In the case of the third gooseberry bush which I illustrate, and which I took from a consignment supplied by a well-known nursery to a friend of mine (at half a crown apiece or £12 10s. a hundred)—this happens to be four years old, green with fungus, and so weak that in its past two years it has made no growth at all. An example like this is a clear indication that the nurseryman has not made the best of his bushes, either by starving them of manure and cultivation, or failing to transplant them from an overcrowded nursery bed. It illustrates very clearly the danger of buying a pig in a poke.

War-time, admittedly, allows relaxations in regard to quality and encourages the imposition of unduly high prices, and some

A bad and a good one-year-old.

A rubbishy four-year-old

few advertisers in the Press have little conscience in exploiting the public. In the autumn of 1941 I was shown an acreage of completely derelict nursery stock which, in the ordinary way, would have gone on to the bonfire, but which a buyer had secured at a knock-out price to sell to the trusting public.

Loganberries and Allied Fruits.

Loganberries, blackberries, boysenberries and the like, are usually raised from rooted tips. The long shoots made in the summer if left to ramble on the ground will develop an enquiring disposition and the ends will become blunt and insinuate themselves into the soil. From each end, by autumn, a mop of white roots will grow and although the original shoot will maintain contact with the parent plant the youngster will throw up a strong shoot from below soil to start a new plant. Plants which have had a year of rooted life will develop a dark fibrous root very different from the succulent white roots of infancy and there should always be a stout, pushful bud or two tucked away among these roots ready to supply robust growths after planting. The two-year-old logan plant is the best to buy and will grow away better than the yearling. It is possible, but not profitable, to raise true loganberry plants from the leaf. A leaf taken in August, whose stalk is firmly inserted into sand in a frame which is kept moist and closed, will, in a very short time, callus over, send out roots, and provide a small plant before the winter.

None of these fruits comes true from seed, except in occasional cases. The blackberry variety Merton Early does come true from seed. Propagation from the plant is essential if the parental characteristics are to be preserved. In buying berry plants of the trailing tribe look for strong growth and an adequate rooting system. If a plump bud can be seen amid the roots, ready to break into new growth, so much the better.

Raspberries.

When estimating the value and condition of raspberry canes for planting the stock should be looked at in summer when the flower is out or the fruit is about; only so can virus disease be noted. This is dealt with under the chapter on raspberries. When buying canes which are leafless one cannot judge the strength of the plant entirely by its root system. The variety Lloyd George, drawn from a nice light loam, will come out with a mat of fibrous root while an even stronger variety such as Norfolk Giant from a heavy soil may have but little fibrous root and will indeed never develop much. In this case one should look for a stout, clean cane, well ripened, not spindly or green and with a fair amount of root. In any case with these fibrous rooted plants only a very small

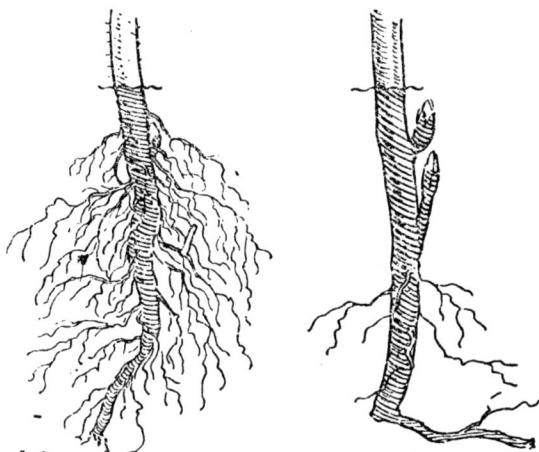

Lloyd George   Norfolk Giant
Raspberry canes pulled from adjoining
rows show that fine canes may grow from
comparatively few roots.

proportion of the original root system is alive and active at
planting time, but from what live root there is, fresh fibres will
soon develop if planting is well done.

Strawberries.

Everyone wants strawberries and there are never enough.
No fruit can be more disappointing if the strain planted is
not sound and prolific. The strength of runners varies with
the different varieties, and size and strength of individual
runners bought for planting also varies according to the position of the runner on the parent plant. Where runners are
"bought-in," having been dug by the grower from the field,
the buyer is at the mercy of the man, or woman, who raises
and bunches the plants. They are usually bunched in twenty-
fives, and it is an easy matter to slip half a dozen smalls into
the bundle, surrounding them with better specimens. If
you are buying by the tens of thousands this is a matter of
little consequence, but where you are paying a fancy price
per hundred, it is no joke. If, therefore, you are shown runners
in bundles, ask to have a bundle opened and examine them for

yourself. See also that the roots are strong and fresh, yellow in colour and not short, dead and black.

Although it does not matter how many runners are raised from a sound strawberry plant, which is not allowed to fruit, it is simpler to limit the runners to ten or a dozen per plant so that they can be easily looked after by the grower. These he either pegs down or inserts into pots of good soil sunk in the row, thus getting a splendid root system. Now when a strawberry runner sends out that long tentative tendril and a plant develops half-way along it and pushes its roots into the soil, the runner continues to run and to lay down fresh plants, but the first runner always has first draw on the sap supply and is some weeks earlier than the others, and so by autumn is a far better plant. Such plants from a good strain are worth almost any price and will pay for planting.

When buying plants which have not received such care and attention see that the central crown is plump and solid. Note also that the old leaves are not unduly covered with leaf spot disease or the young central leaves twisted and deformed by the "crinkle disease." Strength of plant, as we have said before, will vary with variety. Immensely strong plants are provided, for example, by Madam Kooi, an old favourite which is almost unique in that the fruit requires at least two bites, so vast it is (I have picked one of 5½ ounces weight). Equally strong, but of poor quality, is Evesham Unknown or The Huxley, as it is also called. Paxton is now so weak, in some places, that it is dying out, but new strains are being developed and it is hoped that it may stage a come-back. The variety Oberschlesien (which is the German for Upper Silesia) when first introduced over here some twenty years ago was a very robust type, but that also seems to have gone down badly to disease in many places, and its place has been taken by Tardive de Leopold.

To-day you will see Sovereign and Huxley runners advertised in the fruit-growers' papers as (certified). This means that the parent plants have been examined and passed as fit by a Ministry of Agriculture inspector. This is some guarantee of a clean start.

In choosing plants for autumn and spring planting one should always inspect the parent plants during the fruiting season. This allows one time to compare various strains in different places and to form one's own conclusions as to which are best more or less at one's leisure.

IV

PLANTING FRUIT BUSHES

GOOD planting has considerable effect on the early growth and vigour of any tree or bush. It is not enough to dig out a square hole, bundle the roots into it, chopping off any which may overlap the sides, and, having thrown in a mass of clods, to do a shuffle round the bush and expect it to grow. That bush has a long life ahead of it and should be given every consideration. If you have ordered your trees from a distance and are expecting them along at a time when the weather is cold, you should have covered over an open space in the garden with every sort of litter, rubbish, old sacks and so forth that you have available, in order that frost may be kept out and a trench to accommodate your trees temporarily may be got out and filled in again with the soil in the best possible condition.

When the Fruit Bushes Come.

When you have received a consignment of fruit trees by train, beautifully packed in straw as they usually are, meticulously tied with yards and yards of excellent cord, which your fingers positively itch to untie, the yearning can be given full play, for the sooner the trees are out of their packing and in the ground the better. Trees which are left in the bundle owing to severe weather will, at times, give ideal nesting quarters for a fecund mouse, which, having brought forth her family, will proceed to nourish herself on the sappy bark and roots of the trees within the package. I have seen hundreds of trees stood in their bundles near a sheltering hedgerow during a cold spell, which, when unpacked, disclosed roots eaten off and stems nibbled to clean white wood by field mice.

Before undoing the bundle of trees remove the litter which covered the site of your trench and get out a length of trench sufficient to accommodate the trees and see that the soil is finely broken up. Then unpack the trees or bushes and lay them in the trench, covering over the roots with the fine soil. If the weather is not frosty and the tree roots are very dry they can be left in a tub of water for an hour or two or well watered before "heeling in." Press the soil fairly firmly down

among the roots for protection against hard weather, but do
not replace the litter and rubbish which you moved away, as
this may tend to attract mice. If you are laying-by apple,
plum or other trees, lay them in at an angle of 45°, so that
they will not be so liable to blow about. These precautions
are needful only if the weather is cold or the soil too wet
to work nicely.

Writers are apt to emphasise the need for planting only
when the soil is "friable." This is a very nice idea, but some
soils very seldom are friable except in a July drought, and to
my mind the tree which is planted and well staked but whose
roots are not rammed tight home until such time as conditions
allow, is just as well off as a tree in a trench waiting to be
moved. If the holes are waterlogged and the soil like a mud-
pie, as happens when a long cold spell gives place to a sudden
thaw, then, by all means, wait for better times.

Getting Out the Hole.

Do not forget that soil, unless it has been well and truly
worked and manured over a period of years, consists of a
top spit (a spit is a spade's depth) of more or less fertile soil
and below that a much less fertile soil, unaerated and even
sour. If a tree or bush is being planted which demands a
large hole and the ground has not been well manured and
double-dug within the previous year, it is a good plan to lay
aside carefully the top spit of soil when digging the hole and
to dig out the second spit depth, distributing this over the
surface of the soil away from the tree. The tree is then
put into place and the hole is filled in with spadefuls of top
soil taken from near the hole and with the top-spit soil set
aside for that purpose. The hole will then be filled only with
good fertile soil and the poor stuff from below will be able
to weather on the surface and mix in during cultivation.

The Value of Roots.

Some trees have a few straggling roots, others have a mass
of fibrous roots. Usually apple, pear and plum trees from
the nursery will have had their roots roughly severed with a
spade, some being scraped and many broken. This does not
matter a great deal, for in any case only a fraction of the
original complete root system is there and, so long as the
broken roots are trimmed well back, the trees will grow away,
provided that they are firmly planted.

Once, from a bundle of damaged plum trees, I selected a sizeable specimen whose roots had been so badly bitten by mice and rabbits that only a white fang or two remained. My foreman laughed at the idea of trying to grow it. The damaged roots were cut right back almost to the main stem and the tree was planted, staked and the soil around it rammed as hard as the soil round a gatepost. That tree never looked back and grew away as well as the undamaged trees.

There was an American system of close root pruning originated by a Texas grower, called Stringfellow, which recommended cutting off practically all the roots of trees, leaving only short stubs an inch or so long. The tops of the young trees were also cut back very hard. Nobody bothers to do this to-day, but it serves to prove that much of the main root, many of the fibrous roots and practically all the root hairs are dead when a tree, having been dug from its nursery row, bedded for a month or two, lifted and packed and railed, arrives at the garden ready for planting. New root hairs have to grow before new roots can form and before water can be taken up to the buds. For this reason Autumn planting is preferable to Winter and Spring planting, since rooting will have begun before the buds are making a demand on the sap or water supply.

Firm Planting Essential.

To ensure firm planting of a soft fruit bush (which does not, of course, need a stake to steady it) the procedure should be as follows. Having marked out the positions of your various trees with canes or sticks, cut a square hole, taking the stick as the centre, and dig out the soil to the required depth and circumference. Do not leave the bottom of the hole flat, but drop in enough fine soil to mould up into a cone shape so that when the roots are pressed firmly down upon this soft soil the lowest roots will find a resting place without there being any fear of an unfilled hollow beneath them. Continue to fill in the hole, shaking the tree occasionally while doing so, until the hole is filled to about the half-way mark. Now, taking care not to hit the unburied roots, ram the soil very firmly in the hole with a wooden rammer. Having done this finish filling in the hole with top soil and then ram tight and firm once more. There will then be a considerable depression left round the stem which should be filled in with loose soil and the job is done. After planting any broken branches can be cut out and in early March a good mulch of rotted farmyard manure or compost should be spread around to prevent top soil drying out before the roots have got to work.

I have stressed the importance of ramming; it can hardly be over-stressed. A tree, provided the soil is fairly dry at planting time, should be planted just as firmly as a gate post and then the roots, having pressure to work against, will function to capacity, but unless the soil is in nice condition the ramming can be postponed. In heavy soils the hard ball of soil remains, in some cases for years, presumably until the swelling of roots and stem breaks it up. Young trees, planted early, can be cut back hard and this balances up root and head and makes anchorage easier.

Posts for Loganberries.

Soft fruit bushes, unless grown in fancy shapes such as cordon gooseberries and currants, need no support, though raspberries are all the better for it. For loganberries and others of the trailing tribe support is essential. To keep wire tight straining posts must be employed, and these must be completely rigid and immovable. A post merely driven into the soil cannot support the tension of a strained wire without being stayed. A stay is only effective provided it is also rigid, long enough and set sufficiently high against the post to take the strain. If set too low, especially where the post is not deep-set, it merely provides the fulcrum for a leverage which will tend to lift out the post.

Straining posts for loganberry rows should be of chestnut or ash, 4 ins. in diameter at the top and 8 to 9 ft. long. This will allow for 2 ft. 6 ins. to 3 ft. being in the ground and up to 6 ft. out of the soil. The stay can be much lighter, say 2½ ins. diameter at the top and 6 ft. long. If the bark is peeled off the post's life is doubled.

Having dug out a hole for the post wide enough to allow for comfortable ramming all round, it can be dropped in and well and truly firmed, taking care that the post leans outwards away from the loganberry row about 3 ins. The tightening of the wires will bring it back to the vertical. Now lay your stay out in its approximate position and having noted where the bottom of the stay rests get out a hole about a foot nearer to the post and about 9 ins. or 10 ins. deep, cutting the back at an angle as illustrated in the picture (page 44).

The next thing to do is to cut a deep nick in the top of the post into which the stay will fit, this having been trimmed off at the correct angle. The head of the stay already in place, the bottom end is supported by a brick beneath and so arranged that it also butts up against another brick, the hole in which the bricks lie being altered as required. The stay should now be nailed to the post, using a 4-in. nail and taking care to drill a hole for its entry to avoid splitting the stay. The bottom end of the stay is then earthed in and rammed tight. The post is now ready for wiring as soon as you have repeated the operation at the other end of the row. Holes for wire or eye-bolts should be drilled before erection of posts.

For loganberry rows there should be three or even four wires between the top of the post and the soil, and it is a great convenience to use adjustable screw-eyes at both ends or, anyhow, at one end of the row. These can be had in varying lengths and with 4-inch straining posts 12-in. eyes will be needed. A hole should be drilled to receive each screw eye and the screw should be pushed through just far enough to slip on a washer and engage the nut. The wires can then be fixed to the far end and tightened by hand as much as is possible. When all are in position the nuts can be turned to draw the screw-eye through the post, tightening the wire as it goes.

Raspberries.

Where raspberries are wired less strain is exerted on the post, since it need be no more than 4 ft. or 5 ft. out of the ground, according to the strength of the variety planted and the richness of your soil. Even the stay can be dispensed with if an outsized tent-peg be driven into the earth on the opposite side of the post to that occupied by the stay. Where this type of wiring is employed the two straining posts should incline inwards slightly to allow for the pulling-up effect of the wire between the top of the post and the tent-peg.[1] The connection here should consist of a double wire so that by inserting a stout stick the two wires can be twisted up on the principle of the Spanish windlass. Before doing this a double wire should be stretched tightly between the two

[1] In both the illustrations (pp. 44–5) the exigencies of space tend to cramp the illustration. In the stayed post it is preferable to use a longer stay placed further away from the post. In the strained post the tent-peg should be several feet away from the post in ground which is made as firm as possible.

straining posts along the line of the raspberry canes. Then, having tightened up the end wires by twisting, and while the two main wires along the row are taut, pieces of inch batten, about a foot long, can be used to open up the wires and can

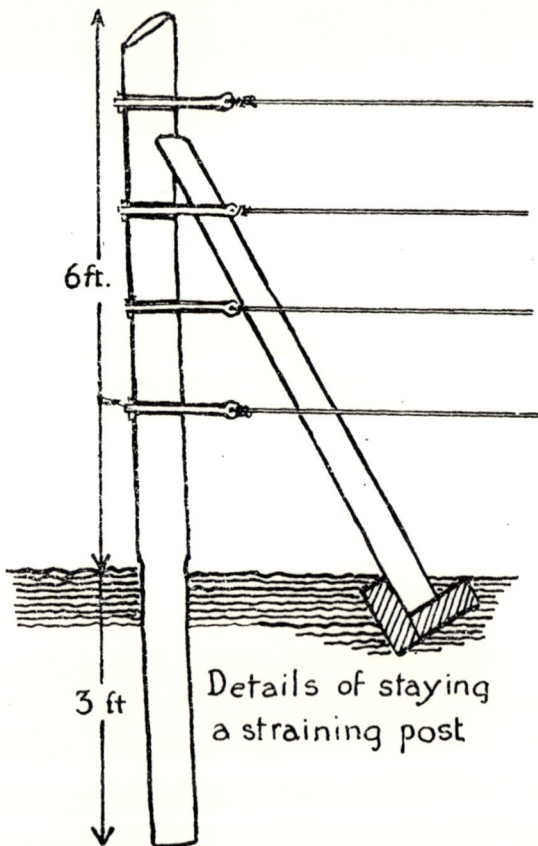

6ft.

3 ft

Details of staying
a straining post

be stapled into position. Where a single wire is preferred the job is even simpler.

To anchor the straining post for a raspberry row the commercial grower prefers to replace the tent-peg with a short log. This is surrounded with a wire loop which is drawn

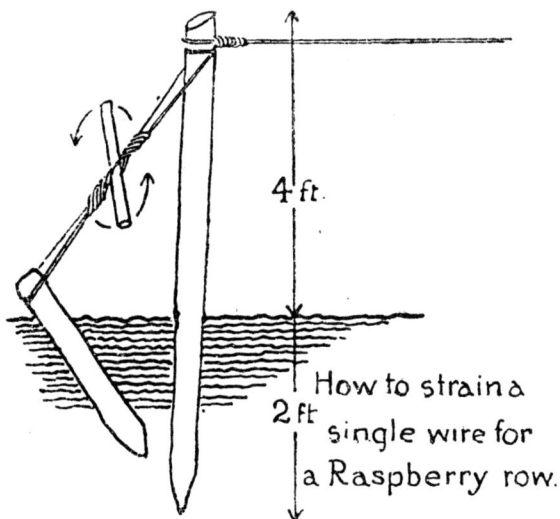

4 ft.

2 ft

How to strain a
single wire for
a Raspberry row.

tight, the log then being buried a couple of feet below soil
level and the free end of the wire attached to the top of the
post holding it firmly in position against the pull of the wire
along the raspberry row.

Blackberries.

The strong-growing Himalaya Giant, which can make shoots
over 20 ft. long in a season, is at its best trained along the
top of a cleft chestnut pale fence. It is then within reach
and also acts as an impassable barrier against animals and
human beings. If trained as a loganberry really heavy wire
and stout posts should be used.

V

BLACKBERRIES, LOGANBERRIES AND HYBRIDS

THERE are more than a hundred species of blackberries native to England, and probably over a thousand if the world were searched for them. Even to-day a hedgerow may exhibit a berry of unusual earliness, size or flavour, and such are worth marking, removing in winter and cultivating.

The gardener who is not well acquainted with the habits and growing powers of blackberries should be careful what he plants. I once planted a Himalaya Giant in a small garden and in three years' time it became quite obvious that either the house or the blackberry would have to be moved, since 20-ft.-long shoots which root at the tip as soon as they touch soil, and progress in annual leaps and bounds, do not assort well with mixed gardening. There are, however, much thriftier varieties and a choice should be made which suits their allotted place in the garden. For all cultural operations, save picking the fruit, strong thorn-proof gloves are needed when dealing with these canes as their spines and thorns are shockingly sharp and often difficult to remove.

Soil.

Both blackberries and loganberries have a spreading, fibrous root system and need a regular, and ample, water supply. Blackberries, which grow so admirably in Devon in parts where the annual rainfall is 60 ins. and over, will flourish in the ditches of lanes which are super-saturated for much of the year, but the berry tribe as a whole, though fond of moisture, needs drainage. Once I advised the removal of a large block of cultivated blackberries growing on a thin soil of flints and clay overlying chalk. They were planted on a rounded hillock and extended down the side of this into a shallow valley. In dry years the plants at the top of the hillock collapsed with drought and in frosty years the plants in the valley were cruelly cut. The survivors in the middle section were never able to carry the field to a profit.

Raising Plants.

Blackberries, logans and most of the hybrid berries will, if allowed, develop an intrusive blunt end to the tips of their summer growth which will root into the soil before autumn and develop into a plant. This can be detached in early spring and grown on for a year and moved as a two-year-old. Commercial raisers encourage the tips to root by pushing them into holes while in full growth and firming the soil about them. The growth soon turns to rooting activity and plants may be so started from the end of June through July and August.

Planting.

These berries can be planted out as one- or two-year-olds. The roots are nicely spread out in the hole dug to receive them, taking care when firming them not to damage the fat buds which lie tucked away against the main stem. Cut back to a sound bud about a foot above soil level in spring and mulch with well-rotted manure or compost.

Training.

Anyone who has a stretch of chestnut pale and wire fencing can make it pay dividends by planting along it, at 15-ft. intervals, canes of the Himalaya Giant Blackberry. Such fences are usually 3 ft. 6 ins. to 4 ft. high, and if additional

Black-berries trained on the Rope system. Fruiting cane is shown as leafless cane.

posts can be inserted so that a stout wire at 5 ft. can be added, the arrangement is excellent; cattle will not touch the canes and the fence is rendered entirely unclimbable by anything less than a tank. I have measured single shoots which, in a season, produced canes 3½ ins. in circumference and carried up to 70 ft. of new combined side and extension growths. Since the main-stem thorns are really formidable and the barbs on the midrib beneath the leaf will tear a pair of flannel trousers to shreds, it is just as well that the fruit is borne on long shoots which hang well away from the main canes.

This particular fruit can be grown on the rope system as in commercial cultivation, but it is not really a fit subject for the small garden unless there happens to be a fence available of the type suggested.

Other varieties of blackberry, less formidable in type but better flavoured and equally fruitful, can be trained as suggested for loganberries or, instead of the fan method, the rope method of training can be employed. No more than eight main shoots should be allowed on this system, and two can be run together on each wire as illustrated. Some growers consider that a single cane per wire is enough, but if the plants are growing away well the reduction of cane is apt to force too much fresh growth from the base which is troublesome to control. By using two canes per wire one new cane can always be brought up into place and the older of the existing two cut out.

Training Loganberries, etc.

To do this job really well one requires a deal of room: 10 ft. to 12 ft. between the canes is none too much to allow where growth is really strong, although where growth is poor 6 ft. apart may suffice. The usual system of covering a wire trellis completely over with fruiting canes and allowing the new young canes to lie in a tangled mass below them is not conducive to well-ripened wood, which alone can give a first-class crop next season. Even the system which allows new canes to be tied up to a wire slung beneath the fruiting canes is by no means ideal, because the fruiting wood, in damp situations and particularly in the case of loganberries and some hybrids, is apt to develop a leaf spot disease, the spores from which will fall upon and infect the new cane and leaf directly beneath. One really needs an arrangement which will look after the new canes and keep them above, or at least away from, the fruiting canes. The obvious solution is a system which will allow wide spacing between the plants, using one section for fruiting wood and the other for growing wood, but this does not suit the economically-minded gardener, and so he spreads out the fruiting canes into a V formation, which he limits to the 5-ft. wire, and allows the new canes to come up through the centre, training them temporarily along the topmost wire. On this system three wires are

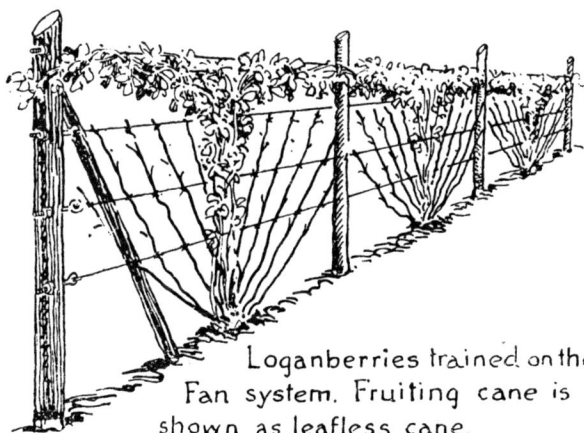

Loganberries trained on the Fan system. Fruiting cane is shown as leafless cane.

necessary, set respectively at 3 ft., 5 ft., and 6 ft. above soil level. Plants should be allowed 10 ft. from each to each as a minimum. In Suffolk in the summer of 1944 I saw a commercial grower's method of training Boysenberries which was new to me: 5-ft. posts had three wires, one at 6 ins. from the soil, one at 3 ft. and the other on the top of the post. The Boysenberry canes, always sparse and leggy, were twisted into a rope and tied in a single bunch to the two wires at an angle of about 45°. All the fruiting shoots were thus condensed into a very small space while the new shoots lay along the lowest wire as they grew during the summer. Plants were set about 8 ft. from each other, but might easily have been closer. Pruning simply consisted in cutting off the rope of shoots after fruiting, selecting enough new wood, twisting the canes together, tying in place and cutting away any surplus canes.

Pruning.

Since, after fruiting, the wood of loganberry and hybrid berries of that type dies and is replaced by the wood of the season's growth, pruning is a simple matter, since it merely consists in cutting out at ground level all the fruited canes as soon after picking is finished as may be convenient. Where canes are fruited on the fan system the ends are kept cut back to the level of the top wire and, when these are removed and the new canes are in place, these in turn are cut back to the level of their predecessors. Where the rope system is used there is no point in allowing a great deal of overlapping of cane from adjoining plants, and, since these ends are usually unripe, they are best cut back when moving buds show live wood to cut to.

Blackberry pruning is a different matter, since canes will live and fruit for several years, and only dead wood and the wood older than two years needs to be removed annually in order to allow strong new growths to take its place. The drastic thinning out of the tender young basal shoots of all the berry tribe early in the season is far better practice than letting a surplus grow for removal in the autumn. Where this is done better and bigger fruits will result, and the reduced amount of cane will benefit.

Other Possibilities of Training.

Berries of the weaker type (not the Himalaya Giant) can be grown up a post on the lines of a rambler rose, and there is no reason why half a dozen or more varieties should not be grown up posts or over pergolas, along chains, or poles, or over arches as productive and decorative specimens. Some forty years ago at Slinfield Manor, near Basingstoke, there used to be a long path arched over by canes of the Cut-leaf Blackberry which made a pleasant change from cordon apples or pears, and from fruiting to the fall of its coloured leaves was a thing of sheer beauty.

For specimen berries grown on such lines the choice might include: The Youngberry, Bedford Giant, The Veitchberry, Phenomenal Berry, Loganberry, King's Acre Berry, John Innes Blackberry, Cut-leaf Blackberry and Boysenberry. This would give a supply of fruit from early July till late October. The Himalaya Giant, in view of its "panzer-like" activities and insistent demand for more "*lebensraum*" (it actually is of German origin), is purposely omitted from this list.

Manuring.

All these fruits crop very heavily, and if size of berry and weight of crop are to go together they must be well fed. The water content of the soil is important and in drought spells, particularly where stone is near the surface or soil is shallow, it is not uncommon to see canes of the stronger growing varieties collapse completely from lack of water. Heavy, dressings of farmyard manure is the best manuring systems but the compost heap can also be drawn upon and its virtues supplemented with good nitrogenous organic manures such as meat and bone, dried blood, chicken manure, hoof meal and so on. Potash being at present unobtainable for fruit, the ashes from the bonfire should replace it.

Varieties of Blackberry and Hybrid Berries.

Bedford Giant: Said to be of Veitchberry parentage. The best early ripening variety. Fruit is large, very black and juicy and of good flavour. Ripens early July onwards. Growth is strong. Plants need 12 ft.

Himalaya Giant: Of mid-European origin. Fruit medium to large, rather seedy but excellent for cooking and preserving. A heavy cropper and very strong grower. Needs 15 ft. to 20 ft.

Cut-leaved or Parsley-leaved Blackberry: Of English origin. Large fruit of fine appearance and flavour. Growth strong and a heavy cropper. Needs 10 ft. to 12 ft.

John Innes: Of English origin. Fruit is large, sweet and juicy. This is a late variety which crops heavily into October. Growth strong. Needs 12 ft.

Merton Thornless Blackberry: A new berry ripening throughout August and September. Fruits are up to 1 in. in diameter. Needs 12 ft. Obtainable from the John Innes Institution, Merton Park, London, S.W.19 (Plate II).

Loganberries and Hybrid Berries.

Loganberry: Of American origin; said to be a cross between a raspberry and a blackberry. Fruit is large and ripens through red to purple. Excellent for cooking and preserving. Those who like acid fruits say that it can be eaten for dessert when fully ripe. Plant at 10 ft. to 12 ft. where growth is good, 6 ft. where weak.

Phenomenal Berry: An improved type of logan ripening a few days later. Treat as a logan.

Lowberry: Of Californian origin. Grows like a loganberry but its 2-in.-long fruits are black and have none of the acidity of the logan. Plant at 12 ft.

King's Acre Berry: Of English origin. Is more like a compact type of blackberry than anything else. Fruit is conical and black, ripening from early July, and fruits part from the core as a raspberry does. An excellent cooking variety. Plant at 12 ft.

Veitchberry: Of English origin. A cross between a blackberry and a raspberry. Fruit is large, of good flavour and mulberry coloured. A strong grower and a heavy cropper. Plant at 12 ft.

Boysenberry: Of American origin. Said to be a cross between blackberry, raspberry and loganberry. Colour deep mulberry. Fruit very large, juicy and acid. Excellent cooked. Canes are thin but growth is strong. Crop is not very heavy. Plant at 12 ft.

Japanese Wineberry: Decorative enough to enjoy a post to itself. Berries are bright orange and edible. Plant at 8 ft. to 10 ft.

Worcester Berry: This is said to be a cross between a gooseberry and a black currant and forms a sizeable bush, carrying a fruit in clusters like small dark gooseberries. Actually it is a true Ribes variety. A heavy cropper and a strong grower. Plant as a bush allowing 6 ft.

The Youngberry: This is of Californian origin and said to be a cross between a dewberry and a loganberry. Fruit is large, reddish-black and juicy. Flavour is very good. Plant at 10 ft. apart.

Pests.

The Raspberry Beetle (described under that fruit) attacks all the blackberry and logan tribe and must be controlled with derris dust or wet spray.

Greenfly will cover the flowering shoots in the bud stage, particularly in the case of Himalaya Giant. The tips of growing canes are also attacked. The pest is easily controlled with a Nicotine and soap wash or Nicotine and a wetting agent in water ($\frac{1}{2}$ oz. of pure nicotine to 8 gallons of water plus the recommended amount of the particular wetting agent.

If soap is used 1 lb. of soft soap is required). Tar oil spraying in winter will prevent an aphis attack.

The caterpillars of the Shoot Moth sometimes attack tips of growing canes and spin up the young leaves with web. The tight bunches of leaf are easy to notice and the offenders can be found by unravelling the leaves and "liquidated" by pressure between the forefinger and thumb.

The Raspberry Moth also offends at times on the same lines and should be dealt with as above.

Fungus Diseases.

Cane Spot. This trouble also attacks the raspberry. It is noticeable first on the fruiting cane and later on the leaf as a purple spot and spreads from there on to the new seasonal growth, especially where this is lying directly beneath infected leaves. Bare, dead ends of shoots are a spring sign of last year's infection. In so far as is possible new young cane should be kept well away from the fruiting cane. It should never lie below the infected shoots since spores will easily and rapidly infect the young new leaf.

The latest Research Station recommendation is the application of not less than two sprays: (1) A mid-May, that is pre-blossom, spray of Bordeaux Mixture (2: 3: 50); (2) End of June (when the beetle is about) using a combined colloidal copper at maker's recommended strength (Bouisol is of this type) with Derris or D.D.T. added to take care of beetle and a wetting agent or spreader.

A simpler but less effective method is to dust lightly with Bordeaux dust (as used against potato blight). This can be put on several times before flowering and after the fruit is picked and will act as a preventive against infection.

The above are the troubles most likely to afflict the amateur grower.

VI

THE BLACK CURRANT

WE live in an age of Vitamin appreciation and the value of
Vitamin C was officially recognised in 1795 when lime juice
was issued to the Navy as a preventative of scurvy when
deprived for long periods of proper supplies of fruit and green
vegetables. It is a mistake to imagine that we must have
lime or orange juice for our Vitamin C, for while it is true
that oranges are an excellent source of supply our own home-
grown black currants offer a better one. The ratio of Vitamin
C in orange juice is only 60 as compared with 160 in the
black currant. Red currants contain but a quarter as much
as black, while white currants appear to be innocent of all
Vitamin C, so, for your health's sake, plant black currants
while retaining room for a few red currants for the absolutely
essential jelly to go with the mutton.

Soil.

Black currants love manure. They will succeed equally well
on deep rich sands and on good heavy loams. They do not
appreciate thin light chalky soils, but, if sizeable holes are
dug at planting time and the poor soil replaced by top soil, or
good imported soil, bushes can be grown almost anywhere.
A firm roothold is essential, and, in the writer's experience,
very high land seldom produces long-lived bushes.

Black currants are so easy to raise that there is no excuse
for retaining the old and unprofitable specimens which are all
too common in most gardens.

While ten years has been given as the average profitable life
of a black currant bush I recall a plantation of over thirty
years of age from which an average of over twenty pounds of
fruit per bush had been picked in a frost-free year.

There are over twenty varieties of black currant to choose
from, and provided the strain is sound all are good. One can
begin the season with the early Boskoop Giant, carry on with
that popular old favourite Seabrook's Black, and finish in
August with Daniel's September. Names which may seem
strange to the amateur, such as Wellington's Triple X and

Davison's Eight, are choice selections from seedlings or stock raised by well-known growers. Westwick Choice and Hilltop Baldwin are others. The last-named has given me the heaviest crop during the past ten years.

The Importance of Sound Stock.

Far too many of the country's currant bushes are useless cumberers of the earth. Some consist of a few scrawny shoots springing from a gnarled stem. Others show the change of leaf-shape and veining known as "nettle-head" or reversion (q.v.), while it is uncommon to find an elderly bush in many private gardens which is not infested with big-bud mite and so deprived of most of its fruitful possibilities.

To raise good bushes and to grow good fruit one must buy the very best obtainable stock and keep it up to standard. Specious advertisements and cheap offers will not help you here. Go to the very best commercial nurserymen (there are not many of them), pay the price, and make a sound beginning.

Raising Bushes.

Only strong healthy bushes should be used for striking cuttings. Clean young shoots arising from the previous season's wood, or stout suckers thrown up from the soil around the base of the bush are chosen, and cut off clean at their base. No buds are removed, as the black currant bush (unlike the red) is best grown from a stool and not from a stem or leg.

The cuttings, which can be taken from October to January, but the earlier the better, are pushed into the soil to a depth of about 6 ins. to 8 ins. Two buds should show above the soil and the cuttings can either be cut back to these buds after insertion or cut to length before planting.

To plant the cuttings choose a well-manured and deeply-dug piece of ground and a nice, dry day. Set out a line and along it make a slit with a spade. The cuttings can then be pushed into the slit, allowing 6 ins. between each. Rows should be 18 ins. to 2 ft. apart to allow for easy cultivation. As each row is filled the soil should be firmed on both sides of the cutting rows with a rammer. A 5-ft. length of 2-by-2-in. wood will do admirably. After frosts the thawing out of the top layer of soil will lift the cuttings, which as yet have no root to anchor them. When this has occurred

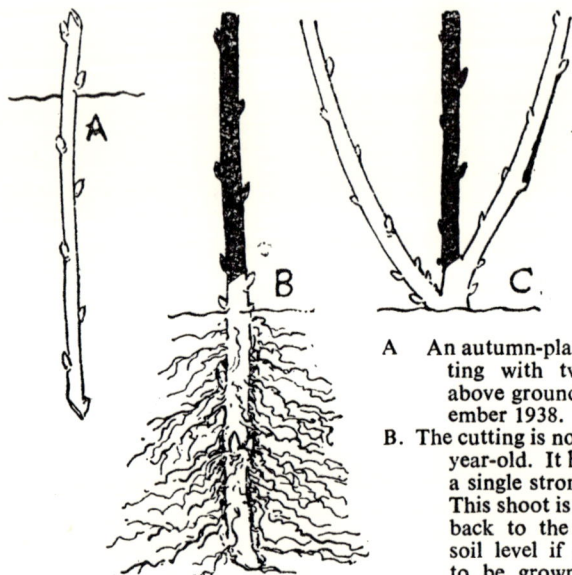

A　An autumn-planted cutting with two buds above ground. November 1938.

B.　The cutting is now a one-year-old. It has made a single strong shoot. This shoot is cut hard back to the buds at soil level if intended to be grown on for a two-year-old. If planted out in its permanent quarters it should be cut down after planting. November 1939.

C.　As a result of the hard pruning our currant—now a two-year-old —has grown three strong shoots. If it is to be transplanted as a two-year-old it should be planted out and all the shoots cut back again. If it was planted out as a one-year-old only one strong shoot need be cut off and the remaining two will be allowed to carry fruit, in the summer of 1940.

In each case black indicates what to cut away.

the cuttings must be pushed home again to ensure contact between the cutting base and soil, but if well pushed down at planting time this should not be necessary until winter has gone. Mulching the cutting rows during early summer with old, rotted manure, compost or grass from the lawn mower, and watering in drought spells are all worth while.

By such manuring, and by keeping down weeds with regular hoeing, you should have strong young bushes a year after setting out the cuttings. These will carry from one to four shoots apiece, but the number of shoots is of no importance, since all will be cut off when the bush has been planted in its permanent quarters.

Bushes can be planted out as two-year-olds if preferred but in that case all the shoots should be cut back hard after planting to encourage strong new growths. Little—if anything—is gained by planting three-year-olds and the one- or two-year bush is to be preferred. Fruit should never be expected during the summer following planting. Even if a little was allowed to develop on unpruned branches it would be poor stuff and the check to growth would be pronounced.

Black currants can also be raised very easily by taking soft wood cuttings in May. At this period the buds of the growing tips of the shoots which are taken are free of Big-bud mite. It is sound policy to dip the shoots, which need only be 4 ins. long, in a nicotine and soap wash. After this they should be planted 2 ins. deep in a cold frame and kept shaded until root action is established. In a few months they can be moved and planted out. The same system of raising soft wood cuttings (there must be no ripe or last season's wood on them) can also be used for many plants and trees. Lilac cuttings can be taken when the bushes are in bloom and be struck on these lines.

Manuring the Fruiting Bush.

The black currant can make use of a great deal of manure and some commercial growers add inches of rotted vegetable matter to their plantations every year. If good, rotten farm-yard manure is available one need seek no further. If it cannot be obtained then one must use compost (q.v.), reinforced with organic nitrogenous manures such as dried blood, hoof and horn, guano and bone meal. The two last named contain not only nitrogen but phosphate, and in the case of guano, potash in addition.

Where chickens are kept their droppings can be used with grass mowings to form a compost on the soil, and if the dressing be repeated at intervals through the season, very good results will be had. Although eminent scientists recommend the use of such inorganic manures as sulphate of ammonia and other forms of nitrogen, the organic or natural types of manure are very much to be preferred. Lime is not needed, and, in the writer's opinion, is not beneficial to this fruit.

Cultivation.

As the black currant roots freely all around its base at soil level, deep, close digging must at all times be avoided.

To make maximum root growth a bush or tree must be firmly anchored. Without maximum root growth one cannot expect maximum shoot production or fruiting. During the growing period, from April to the end of September, weeds should be kept down completely. Continuous, shallow hoeing will attend to all annual weeds, while docks and deep rooters, such as dandelion, should be dug as soon as they are seen and not cut off.

To gain very early fruit plant a few bushes of early varieties, such as Boskoop Giant and Mendip Cross, in a sunny sheltered corner. For sheer size plant against a west wall, select a few branches, and train fanwise. Attend to watering and expect currants as large as cherries or almost.

Pruning.

Pruning is simple provided that you encourage ample growth. After planting out a one- or two-year-old bush, all the branches are cut off just above soil level. Do not attempt to fruit even one branch. During the summer in the first year of planting a nice growth of young shoots should develop and by autumn a bush will have arrived. When the leaf has

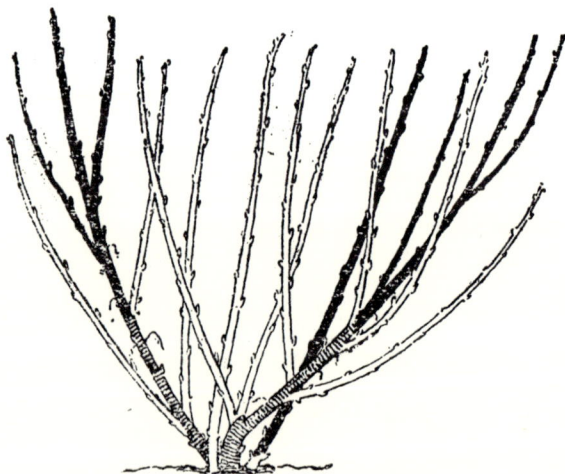

THE SAME BUSH IN 1942.

Two-year-old wood is shaded. Wood for removal is black.

fallen, which indicates completion of development for the season, cut off half the new growths to soil level, leaving the remaining shoots to carry their first crop. From these cropping shoots a number of strong growths will develop ready to fruit next season; new shoots will also spring from the soil.

So much for first and second prunings; your third-year pruning will consist in the removal of possibly two of the two-year-old shoots which have fruited, again cutting down to soil level if there is plenty of new growth in the bush. If you feel that the strength of the bush justifies it you may leave perhaps two or three growths on the two-year-old wood instead of cutting down to soil level. Also cut clean down to soil level a proportion of the strong sucker shoots which have come up from the ground around the base of the bush.

This hard cutting is all aimed at encouraging the bush to form itself into a regular cluster of strong young growths mainly supported by their own roots. It is bad economy to produce a bush on a leg, for very little top growth can be expected on so limited a root system. After the third year the grower should be expert enough to decide for himself what should be cut out and what should remain.

Picking.

A good commercial picker encourages sharp but robust finger-nails so that the strig, or stalk, upon which the currants are set can be nipped off by a sideways pull bearing their fruit intact. Currants must be picked dry if they are to travel to market for retail sale, and if near ripe should never be railed in anything bigger than a six-pound chip basket. The commercial grower very often picks when only a proportion of the fruit is black, some a dusky red and an odd currant or two unashamedly green. This allows for a few days between picking and selling, which is a convenience to distributor and retailer. For home use the riper they are the better, but, if topped-and-tailed, as all good jam makers insist, they are easier to handle on the strig than "milked" from it.

Pests and Diseases.

At least one spray is a vital necessity in black currant growing. Old gardeners will grumble that "My father (who died of the small-pox) never sprayed his black currants," but prevention is better than cure, and spraying, to prevent a greenfly attack on the black currant bush, is just as needful as is vaccination to prevent small-pox in the human race.

A greenfly attack curls up the top leaves of the growing shoots, dwarfs and distorts growth, and covers leaves and fruit below the colony with sticky honeydew. A bad infestation is a really nasty mess. Winter spraying with Tar-oil prevents all this and is a sound economy.

Tar-oil, also known as Winter Wash, is pleasant enough to use. It has a mild carbolic smell, little or no caustic effect on the hands or eyes, save when used at high concentrations or for long periods, and is normally diluted with twenty times its own bulk of water and can be applied with a stirrup pump, or a garden syringe. It has the property of killing the egg of the greenfly which is laid on the shoot in the autumn ready to hatch out in the spring. Tar-oil also has a definitely invigorating effect on the bush in addition to ridding it of all mould, fungus and lichen.

Other Insect Pests.

Occasionally on the black currant bush leaves small, green, active bugs may be observed which run hurriedly out of sight. They are often confused by the amateur with greenfly but are known to the entomologist as the Lygus Bug, one of the Capsid Bugs. These bugs puncture the leaves and shoots while feeding and interfere with normal shoot growth. Where a hundred or so are busy on a bush the check to growth is considerable, and the innumerable punctures on the top leaves of the growing shoots cause the bush to take on a yellowish hue as compared with the vivid green of a healthy bush. It is possible to control this pest completely by using a Petroleum Oil wash containing D.N.C. (Dinitro-cresol) or with a mixed Tar-oil and Petroleum wash, applied in February. This will control both capsid and aphis, but unless capsid is known to be present and doing damage a winter Tar-oil wash is all that should be given. DDT dust in early summer is also very effective.

Occasionally weevils do minor damage to the leaf, and of late years in a few isolated places a midge has caused some damage to nursery stock, but neither of these do much harm in the garden.

Really severe attacks by caterpillars are rare but minor attacks are common. There are two methods of controlling these pests; by spraying with poisonous Arsenate of Lead wash or by using a Derris wash which, while very toxic to caterpillars, is harmless to humans and is generally obtainable from the horticultural chemists or sundriesman.

Big-bud Mite.

Most elderly black currant bushes suffer from this microscopically small pest which exists by tens of thousands in a single bud (Plate V). There are very few cottage gardens where the black currants are not cruelly infested, and as the pest drifts from one garden to the next a Big-Bud Order would be far more to the point than the unobserved Silver Leaf Order is to plum-growing. To the uninitiated the promising big buds suggest bounteous supplies of fruit, but, in fact, all that emerges from the distorted trusses are millions of mites seeking fresh buds and pastures new. Where young trees show a few swollen buds, careful picking-off and destruction of the buds will help to keep the pest down, but where any considerable number of bushes are grown and are likely to become infested, spraying with Lime-Sulphur must be undertaken. To estimate when spraying simply must be undertaken, allow no more than one-third of the buds to be "big." The time to do this is when the leaf is "no bigger than a shilling," and the strength of the wash, as recommended in most fruit growing books, is 1 gallon of Lime-Sulphur to 11 gallons of water. In the case of sulphur-shy varieties, such as Edina, Goliath, Monarch, Victoria and Davison's Eight, a dilution of 1 gallon to 25 gallons of water is recommended. These are both rather heroic doses, and at 1 to 11 severe scorching results. Although the truss will survive and fruiting will not be affected by the scorching, the whole bush is left very much exposed to frost damage at a very critical period in its season, and regular annual spraying, using 1 gallon of Lime Sulphur to 50 gallons of water, should be strong enough to keep the mites under sufficient control with far less damage to youn leaf.

Reversion.

This is the most serious of all the pests which attack the black currant. The insidious invasion of the bush will begin with a single branch, spread to others, and in two or three years the whole bush will be involved, with the complete and final destruction of its cropping power.

In the average garden or allotment, especially where black currants have been neglected for years and are infested with

Big-bud Mite, a close examination of the bushes is likely to disclose the fact that some look different to others (Plate III). The difference will lie in the general colour and appearance of the leaf. On a reverted bush the foliage is of a darker green.

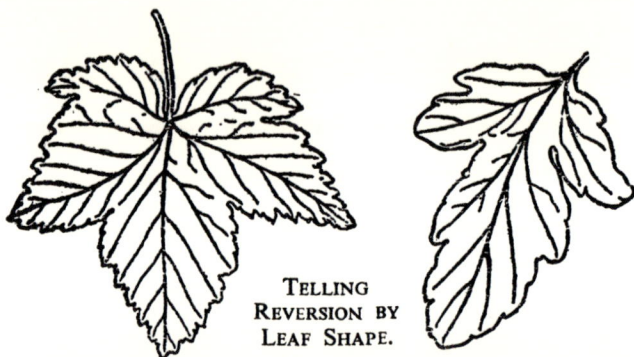

TELLING
REVERSION BY
LEAF SHAPE.

A leaf from a sound bush will show five or six veins on each side of the main leaf divisions.

A leaf from a badly "reverted" bush. The five veins to the leaf divisions have shrunk to three.

The leaf, normally even in shape with a sharply serrated edge, has become simplified. The veins, which supply each section of a sound leaf with its needed moisture, are fewer in number, while in the flowering stage the beautiful lavender bloom which tints the back of the blossom has been replaced by a ginger red. When the flowers of the sound bushes have set and the green fruits are developing nicely those on the reverted bushes have mostly stripped off, leaving only an occasional, undersized specimen behind. By fruit-picking time the badly reverted bush looks completely alien to its fellows with distorted leaves and the typical "nettle-head" formation of the shoots. The only place for such a specimen is the bonfire.

There is no remedy for the disease once it is established. Cutting the bush down to soil level, as has been suggested for Big-bud Mite (quite unsuccessfully), and allowing a whole new bush to spring up will not benefit. The trouble is now known to be a virus disease. The virus itself has not been isolated and there is no clear evidence that the disease is spread by any other mode than by Big-bud Mite and by grafting (an operation only practised by research workers). The grower's

first step in control therefore must be in the direction of the
Big-bud Mite.

The control of aphis by Tar-oil wash, or aphis and capsid by
Tar-oil and Petroleum combined in February, and the regular
attack on Big-bud mite with Lime-Sulphur wash in spring, are
routine measures which must be observed if healthy bushes
are to be retained. In addition to pest control regular
manuring and reasonably hard pruning to ensure good growth
and the replacement of old wood will help to ward off infection.

The diagnosis of reversion by examination of the leaf and
its veins is not always applicable where a proportion of the
leaves or even single branches are concerned. Especially is
this the case when suspicious-looking leaves occur on young
bushes where the growing tip of a shoot has been broken off
and side shoot buds have been energised into growth. What
is known as False Reversion may occur then, but by the
following season the trouble will have disappeared.

This account of a pest may sound rather alarming. In
twenty-five years of black currant growing I have worked a
plantation where several acres of black currants over thirty
years old never showed a Big-bud or a reverted bush. I have
farmed others where the normal span of eight to ten years
of productive life were brought to an untimely end by reversion. In my own garden I have never had a reverted bush
unless the author himself may be so unjustly described. So,
one can realise that it is not everybody's trouble. Freedom
from reversion is dependent mainly on the purity of the stock
from which cuttings were taken to raise bushes. Indiscriminate propagation from stock which is not carefully and
intelligently "rogued" is certain to carry reversion. Commercial growers buy from other growers or nurseries whose
"cutting stools" and two-year-olds are inspected annually by
trained experts from the Ministry of Agriculture. "Certified"
stocks are the safest stocks to plant from.

Varieties.

There are, to-day, a considerable number of varieties to
choose from, and more continue to be produced. Cotswold
Cross and Mendip Cross are two at present on trial, and the
latter may prove to be as early, or even earlier, than Boskoop
Giant which, up-to-date, has held first place. Taking the
catalogues of two good nurserymen the following sorts are

listed and should offer choice enough to anyone save the variety hunter.

Boskoop Giant: Makes a large spreading bush. Very early to ripen. Fruit large and quality good.

Mendip Cross: A new currant of good size. It is about as early as Boskoop but a heavier cropper.

Raven: A heavy cropper with a long bunch and a large berry.

Seabrook's Black: A strong grower. A very heavy cropper. Fruit not so large as some but quality tip-top.

Wellington XXX: A modern commercially-favoured variety of good quality.

Victoria: A clean grower with a large and good berry.

Davison's Eight: A strong grower. A very large berry and a heavy cropper. Quality good.

Baldwin: A strong grower, only where soil is rich. A heavy cropper which will hang late (Plate IV).

Westwick Choice and Westwick Triumph: Both of recent introduction by the raiser of Davison's Eight. Heavy croppers and of good quality.

Daniel's September: The latest variety grown. A good cropper and berries large and well flavoured.

Where choice is limited and the area to plant small, Seabrook's Black is often recommended as the best variety for the amateur. Though fruit is smaller than that of some other varieties it makes up for that in flavour and is well liked by the jam-maker and the canner. In my own garden, in rich loam, Baldwin (Hilltop strain) has always proved to be the heaviest cropper of all. Boskoop Giant and Davison's Eight have always carried the largest fruits. Where there is room for three, Boskoop Giant, Seabrook's and Daniel's September will cover the season. There is no need when planting this fruit to worry about cross fertilisation since all are self-fertile. All that is needed to secure a good crop is freedom from aphis and from frost with plenty of visiting bumble-bees when the flowers are out.

VII

RED AND WHITE CURRANTS

THESE are an entirely different proposition to black currants. The black currant is fed and pruned to promote a liberal supply of young new wood, but the red and white currants are fed and pruned to induce fruitfulness from old wood, with as little production of young wood as may be needed to ensure fruit buds.

Soil and Site.

A nice, easy-working loam suits these currants best, but any soil can be brought into condition to produce good bushes. A sunny site is essential, particularly at ripening time, and the partial shade which suits the black currant is not appreciated.

When young and growing strongly the new shoots of some varieties are inclined to break away at the base, the wood being very brittle, and where the site is a windy one the protection afforded by a few wattle hurdles is valuable.

The best distance to plant bushes is at 6 ft. apart, and eight permanent fruiting branches are enough to allow to each bush. When grown against a wall as single cordons—a popular type of training—12 ins. to 18 ins. apart is the usual distance to plant. By using a North wall the fruit will hang late and its period can be extended considerably.

Raising Bushes from Cuttings.

Although some varieties of Red currant are liable to a type of "reversion" or blindness of shoots which produce some leaf but no fruit (Fay's Prolific is an offender in this respect) they are not afflicted by the same reversion virus which attacks their black brothers. Since the blind shoots are usually stunted they are unlikely to be chosen as cuttings and the risk of raising further blind specimens is avoided. Some strains, however, seem to be predisposed to this trouble.

Because the red currant is grown upon a leg any sucker shoots are firmly discouraged, beginning at the time when the cuttings are prepared for striking. Shoots of sound, ripe wood about a foot or a few inches longer are taken in early autumn and all buds save the top four or five are removed. In some

c

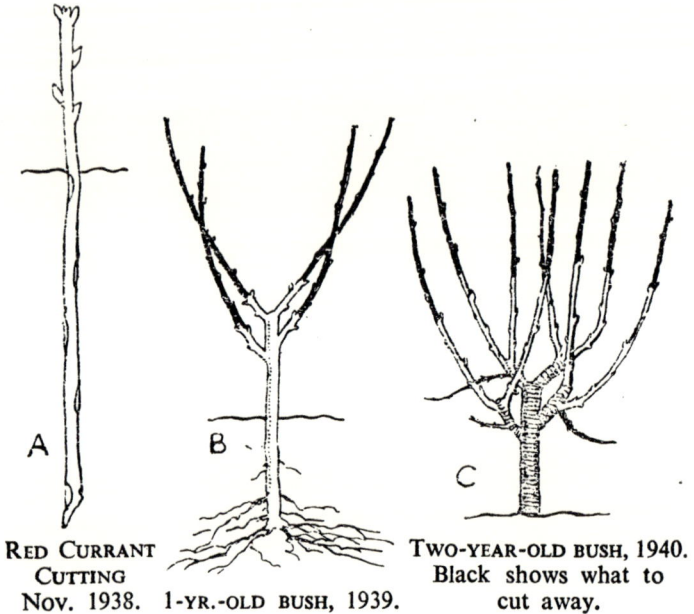

RED CURRANT   TWO-YEAR-OLD BUSH, 1940.
CUTTING   Black shows what to
Nov. 1938. 1-YR.-OLD BUSH, 1939.   cut away.

gardens die-back or botrytis (see p. 85) makes it advisable
to grow gooseberries and red and white currants as stools
and not on a stem. An attacked shoot or branch does not
then involve the whole bush. To grow the currant as a stool
all the buds are left on the cutting. It will be recalled that
in raising black currants all the buds are left on, since suckers
are encouraged.) A spade slit is then made along a line and
the cuttings are firmly pushed home to a depth of 6 ins. or
8 ins., leaving 6 ins. between each pair in the row. The
soil is then firmly rammed on both sides of the row to ensure
that pressure of soil around the base of the cutting which is
essential to root action and formation.

Some growers prefer to take their cuttings in autumn and
heel them in in small bundles to plant out in February or
March. In a very severe winter cuttings in the row are apt
to be lifted up by each frost and thaw, and if the cutting is
to start growth this uplift must be remedied by pushing the
cutting back on to a hard bottom. If, however, the cuttings
are taken as soon as leaf is falling in autumn a good callus

and maybe a few roots will have formed and anchored the cutting. The comparative value of planting out the cuttings in a line in autumn or over-wintering them and planting out in spring is decided by the climate of the locality and the preference of the raiser.

Red and white currants for bushes are best grown as two-year-olds, the plants being lifted at the end of the first year. The roots arising from the upper bud scars are cut away, leaving only the lower roots. They are then replanted. By this method a long stem free from sucker shoots is secured.

You can grow single-branched cordon red and white currants in small gardens and lettuces can be planted right up to them. Cuttings with basal buds removed may be set out *in situ* at a foot apart and run up, keeping the leading growth straight and all side shoots pinched back to 4 ins. Pruning is completed to half an inch in winter and the leading shoot cut back by one-third. Birds do not worry the cordon type of currant, being unable to hold on to a vertical shoot easily. Trained on walls currants are apt to be worried by mice.

Pruning.

There are usually enough shoots on a two-year-old bush to allow one to select four shoots evenly spaced from each other. If these four are cut back to three buds from the base the two top buds remaining will break into growth and eight leaders will then be secured. Once established the currants are apt to throw a regular jungle of shoots unless checked. Unwanted strong growths or suckers should be stripped off rather than cut off to discourage fresh growth from the same spot.

It will be noted that while black currants produce their fruit on the previous season's wood, which is left unpruned save for an occasional thinning out and hard cutting back to soil level, the fruiting buds of the Red currant are clustered closely against the old wood around the base of the side shoots which spring from the main branches. Fresh buds are formed here year after year and the fruiting wood of these currants is often of considerable age. In summer the rigid outline of the winter-pruned bush disappears amid a forest of side growth, and these should be summer-pruned in June as the fruit begins to colour, cutting them back to about 4 ins. from the main branch. In order to reduce shock this operation should be spread over several days and not done in one fell swoop. A summer pruning opens the fruit to bird attack; the bushes should be netted after pruning.

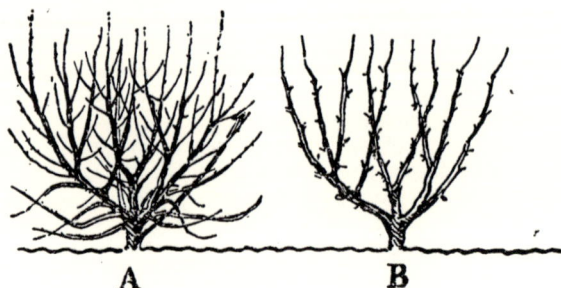

A.   A five-year-old Red Currant Bush before
and (B) after winter pruning.

Winter pruning will follow and the time to begin this will depend upon whether the bushes are grown within a cage, and so are out of the reach of bud-eating birds, or if they are grown in the open and so at their mercy. If the former is the case the bushes can be pruned during winter but in the latter case the branches should be heavily cottoned with black thread and pruned when buds are moving well in late spring. This final pruning consists of cutting all side shoots into two buds (about ½ in.) from the base and in shortening the extension growth of the eight main shoots by half their length or more. As the bush matures the pruning of the extension shoots becomes annually more severe and eventually these are cut back to about ½ in.

Where bullfinches are common (it seems these are reputed to be the sole offenders where gooseberry and currant buds are concerned, though sparrows and chaffinches must be suspect) many buds are taken and the pruning of extension wood must be left until one can be sure which buds will remain, so that one can cut to a bud pointing in the right direction. Summer pruning, indeed all pruning, reduces the strength of the tree and in the case of the cordon red or white currant consisting of a single branch hard pruning is essential in summer and winter to restrict fruitful growth to the one member.

Manuring.

There are differences of opinion regarding the manuring of red currants. Everyone is agreed that thorough preparation of the soil and a generous dressing of stable manure is needed to give a good start to the young bushes, but in later years one school holds that heavy dressings of Sulphate of Potash are essential while others insist that Phosphates are equally or more important. It is certain that an occasional dressing of farmyard or stable manure—say once in three years—and regular applications of from 2 oz. to 3 oz. per sq. yard of raw bone meal in spring is better than inorganic potash and phosphates from the bag. The use of quick-acting nitrogenous manures, while sound enough in the case of black currants, should be translated to slow motion in the case of the red currant, and bone meal will provide that slow output of a moderate nitrogen content which will suit this particular fruit, as well as supplying a generous dose of phosphate. Farmyard manure can always be relied upon to contain a proportion of potash in its most valuable form.

Pests and Diseases.

Red and white currants do not show an infection of big-bud mite in the same way as do black currants; the infection, however, may still be there and buds which fail to open or fruit must be regarded with suspicion. A Lime-Sulphur spray at the recommended concentration for black currants of 1 to 50 can do no harm and where this is being applied to adjoining black currants the reds should be included.

Aphis in two forms will often attack the leaves, but both can be destroyed in winter in the egg stage by spraying with Tar-oil winter wash at the strength recommended by the makers of the particular brand of wash used. The red blisters on the leaves in summer indicate the presence of the currant aphis and a summer infection can easily be stopped with a soap and nicotine or derris spray if necessary.

A Capsid Bug also attacks the red currant, biting and puncturing the leaves and shoots and reducing the growth. This should be dealt with as recommended in the case of black currants. If the winter spray (using not plain Tar-oil but Tar-oil and Petroleum or D.N.C. Petroleum) is not done and the pest develops, a nicotine and soap wash will give fair control, provided that the application is thorough and the ground beneath the bush is included in the spraying. This is necessary because the capsid bug is a nervous and highly-strung insect and at the first alarm will fall and lie doggo until danger is passed, and, unless well wetted, will survive to crawl back up the tree again.

Currant Clearwing Moth is partial to the shoots of red and white currant bushes. It is often seen as a black, white and yellow moth flying about the garden in July and August. Eggs are laid on the shoots in early summer from which caterpillars hatch and bore into the stems, tunnelling up the pithy centres. When branches break off for no apparent reason the weakening caused by such boring is often responsible. The only remedy is to examine shoots when pruning, and, if a hollow blackened centre is seen, to explore it by cutting off inch sections with the secateurs until the offender is found and suitably decapitated.

Coral spot is a fungus attacking old and neglected bushes. Its name is amply descriptive. The fungus gains entry to live wood via a wound in the growing season and any dead wood should be cut away when noticed and burned. There is no remedy save the bonfire, but when a main shoot has had to be removed a junior shoot can usually be promoted to take its place.

Varieties.

The following are a few of the most reliable sorts.

EARLY.

Fay's Prolific: A fine, very large currant, but rather brittle wood.

Earliest of Fourlands: Strong, upright grower and wind-resistant. Large fruit and good cropper.

Versailles: A very heavy cropper but fruit too small.

MID-SEASON.

Houghton Castle: Strong, upright grower. Fruit medium size.

Laxton's No. 1: A vigorous variety, forming a bigger bush than Fay's Prolific. Crops heavier and larger fruit.

LATE.

Laxton's Perfection: Rather weak growth but the largest currant grown. Wood rather brittle.

Raby Castle: Strong upright growth. Fruit medium size. Recommended for cordons.

Rivers' Late Red: Very late. Medium-sized fruit.

Wilson's Long Bunch: Strong grower. Medium-sized fruit (Plate VI).

WHITE CURRANTS.

White Grape, or *White Dutch*: Berries of medium size but a heavy cropper when well manured.

White Transparent: A free bearer with large berries.

There are other currants listed, but these are old favourites with a few new ones added for good measure.

VIII

THE FIG

FIGS may be said to "grow by courtesy" in our climate. Coming as they do from Western Asia, Northern Africa and Southern Europe, they need more light and heat than our summer usually affords. Nevertheless, figs have been grown in England since Thomas à Beckett planted a fig garden at Tarring, in Sussex, in the twelfth century. There, figs have persisted, and in modern times as many as 24,000 top-grade ripe figs have been harvested in a single season.

Aspect.

There is little point in planting figs on any considerable scale save in the southernmost quarter of the country or where the Gulf Stream laps the west coast. Trained trees are grown most successfully on south walls, though, where shelter is really good, they may succeed on an east or west wall. They will not abide growing on open fences or in draughty places. It is an old and tried maxim that the fig should be planted within sight of the sea, and certainly the best crops can be seen around the Worthing district and in Devon gardens, though I recall one old Kentish manor house facing out over the Medway, where the figs were a source of regular and considerable profit to the owner. In North Wales and Anglesey, in sheltered corners, figs succeed admirably.

Soil.

Rich heavy soil spells rank growth and no fruit for the fig, for hard, well-ripened wood is needed for fruit bearing. The ideal soil is warm loam overlying chalk, because, in such soils, tap-roots are discouraged. If the fig is to be kept thrifty in growth and fruitful its root system must be confined to a small space. A bed 2 ft. deep and with no more than 16 sq. ft. to 18 sq. ft. of surface area (i.e. 4 sq. ft. by 4 sq. ft. or 6 sq. ft. by 3 sq. ft. or the equivalent) is plenty large enough. Many will consider a square yard ample.

Having decided on the shape of the bed, and dug out all the soil up to 2-ft. depth, the confining walls should be built with brick or cement and the bottom of the hole filled in solid with a foot of tightly packed brick or slab stone, to allow for drainage but to discourage tap-root formation. When replacing part of the soil plenty of good mortar rubble

should be mixed in. Where more than one fig is planted a
distance of 12 ft. to 15 ft. should separate them.

Propagation of Figs.

Since figs can be raised from cuttings, by layering, or by
lifting suckers, increase is easy. To layer a young fig the
original sucker may be cut down in spring to induce several
young shoots to form. These can be earthed up into a mound
about ten inches high and by the end of the autumn the soil
can be pulled down and young rooted shoots cut off. Cuttings
of well-ripened wood about a foot long, taken in September
and firmly planted in a warm corner, if kept moist, will root
and can be planted out after two years. Suckers may be lifted
in autumn to set out in their permanent quarters. It is a good
plan to buy a fig tree in a pot all ready to train against a wall.
If the pot be 10 ins. to a foot across there is no need to take
the fig tree out of it; pot and tree can be planted as one.
Roots will grow over the top of the pot and can be cut off
when the pot is lifted in late autumn to store in the cellar
ready for setting out again in the late spring.

If a young fig, or a sucker, is planted without any pot
in a prepared site it can still be lifted every few years and
root-pruned in order to keep it thrifty in growth and productive of figs. Manuring of the bed is not necessary, although,
if the soil is really poor, a few handfuls of $\frac{1}{4}$-in. bone can
be worked in at planting time and later, when the tree is
carrying a good crop of fruit in a dry year, a mulch of rotted
manure can be applied, and this and the watering that will
be needed at such times will supply all the encouragement
required.

If, in its early years, the fig growing in the open border
is inclined to throw very strong shoots, these should be stopped
at once by pinching out the tops. As a result they will branch
t freely into short useful shoots.

Training and Pruning.

One often sees the fig relegated to a corner of the walled
garden where it proceeds to throw up enough suckers to
make an impenetrable jungle. This is, of course, unregulated
growth, suckers being allowed to multiply without removal
and the root system to spread without restriction. If one is
going to insist upon the restricted growth which is essential
for fruitfulness one must ensure that the tree does not have
its own way. In a book on fruit, written by a nurseryman of

some distinction in 1872, he tells how he grew his figs regularly in large pots, removing them each autumn as the leaves fell to his cellar where they spent the winter. This regular removal suited the figs admirably and they never had any chance to make rank growth. Incidentally this nurseryman listed nearly a hundred varieties of fig for sale!

To-day, cellars are not usual with small or modern houses, but observance of the suggestions embodied in annual removal and protection from frost can be made. Even where the big fig tree is concerned lifting every fourth year can be helpful.

Since the best site for a fig is a wall the best method of training is the fan system. It simply consists in spreading out the shoots and securing them in position. In selecting and limiting the shoots one should try to visualise the fig shoots in full leaf and allow ample room for each shoot or branch. Only with ample room, sunlight and warmth, will a crop of figs mature.

Where figs are grown upon walls in the open in the South of England or under glass an easy method of training without root-pruning or lifting is to allow enough long shoots to form in the season to cover the wall with a full foot space or more between each. These should be spurred in to a single shoot and tied in as a fan. Well below these a few shoots should be headed back so that fresh seasonal shoots are produced to replace the trained-in shoots when they have been cut out after fruiting. The trained shoots as they enter their second season will carry plenty of fruit and should mature one crop outside or two crops under glass in the season.

Dr. Denham, author of that delightful book *The Skeptical Gardener* (by Humphrey John, published by George Harrap & Company, Ltd., London, at 11/-), tells me that he can ripen figs well in Oxfordshire, where he grows them against a wall planted to Iris Stylosa with their roots covered by a slab-stone path.

Fruiting.

The fig's method of fruiting is, at first sight, puzzling. A bearing shoot will carry quite large fine figs on its lower third (C), followed by a crop of very small figs on the middle section (B), and topped by some tiny embryo figs no bigger than peas (A). The large figs are the only ones which the tree can be expected to ripen. Given a long enough and warm enough summer the second size would mature; but the embryo figs at the top are the crop for next season. It will be obvious then that instead of hoping for a double crop the intermediate size figs should be removed in order to allow the first crop to gain size, and the embryos should be protected against frost so that they can get away well next season.

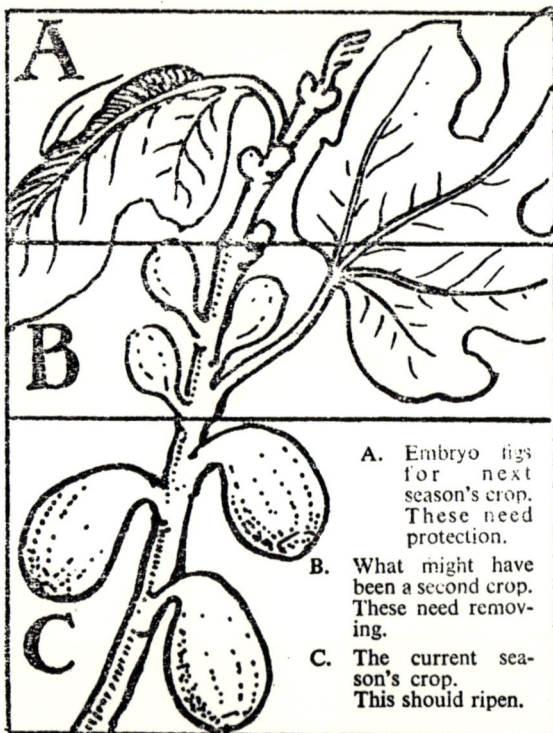

A. Embryo figs for next season's crop. These need protection.

B. What might have been a second crop. These need removing.

C. The current season's crop. This should ripen.

The French have a method of improving the development of figs by removing the wood bud next to the fruit in order to increase the sap flow to the fruit. In June they squeeze the points of bearing shoots so that sap is forced to the fruit. Where earlier ripening is desired a needle dipped in olive oil and pushed into the eye of the fig is said to hasten ripening without injuring flavour. It is agreed by all authorities that to be of full dessert quality a fig must be ripened on the tree.

Barrenness.

It is a common custom in countries where the fig is native or indigenous for the owner to place over his fig tree in the receptive period branches from a wild fig, in order that fertilisation may be effected. While this may be needed where male and female flowers are borne on separate trees, the figs one buys from the nurseryman do not need this attention, and refusal to bear is almost invariably associated with failure to restrict growth. Once the excessive vigour has been toned down fruit will arrive.

Winter Protection.

This may be very necessary in a district which is liable to suffer from low winter temperatures. Where the tree must be left outside, its branches can be free from the wall and bundled together with straw, or a hurdle or two can be made and thatched with straw so that water will run off, and the hurdle secured to the wall. Litter, a foot deep, can be spread around the tree base and over the roots and kept in place. It is suggested that branches of spruce offer first-class protection, as by April, when the tree is needing sun and warmth, the spruce will have shed much of its leaf and will continue to act as a protective agent till the weather permits safe removal. Late April and mid-May are critical times when spring frosts do severe damage, and care should be taken, when the night promises to be cold, that some protection is still available. By so doing the prospects of a good crop are increased.

Varieties.

The four varieties best suited to outdoor culture are probably:

Black Ischia: Hardy and free-bearing. Fruit of medium size. Colour, deep purple. Flavour, very good. Season, early August.

Brown Turkey: Hardiest of all and a good cropper. Fruit, large. Colour, brownish-red, with a blue bloom. Flavour, rich and sugary. Season, August.

White Marseilles: Hardy and free-bearing. Fruit, medium sized. Colour, pale yellow. Flavour, very sweet and rich. Season, August into September.

Brunswick: Hardy and prolific if well fed and watered. The largest fig grown outdoors. Colour, green with dark blue-brown flush and brown dots. Flavour, good. Season, August.

IX

GOOSEBERRIES

AFTER two and a half years of war Cinderella has come into
her own and bushes of this neglected berry are being bought
and sold at prices which can only be described as fantastic.
Of late years the gooseberry would seem to have waned in
popularity. Commercially, a big acreage went out of production some years ago as a result of the jam-makers (who
used large quantities of gooseberry juice to set the sloppier
types of jam) deserting this fruit for apple pectin. Pectin,
which to-day is a by-product of the American apple industry,
is, of course, far cheaper and handier for their purpose. Still
more depressing to the gooseberry has been the increasing
importation of exotic and out-of-season fruits, which, being
available at all seasons of the year, have reduced the ripe and
succulent gooseberry to the position of a nonentity in the
greengrocer's window.

The average amateur, too, appears to have lost interest.
Seventy years ago, when Cotton was king, Lancashire gooseberry fanciers were legion and vied with each other in producing outsize fruits in the red, green, yellow and white
classes. A catalogue of 1872 lists the names of no fewer
than 122 varieties of "show sorts" as compared with the
modern nurseryman's catalogue of no more than thirty or
forty varieties for all purposes. It must have caused Lancashire some annoyance that a variety called London topped
the list up to 1867 with 359 prizes and the highest individual
weight for a berry of 33 dwts. 12 grains, which is a good deal
better than Leveller—the immense, greeny-yellow berry which
still makes high prices in season—was ever able to do.

Soil and Site.

Gooseberries will grow well on almost any soil which is
not waterlogged. I have found them to flourish on deep
sand above the old red sandstone, on lias clay, on light stony
limestone soil, clay on chalk and gravel on clay. Strength of
growth is decided largely by enough water and freedom for
rooting. It is definitely decided and limited by the potash

content of the soil. If this element is short, or almost absent, nothing can be done to induce growth until the deficiency has been made good. I recall a patch of Lancer—a fine green berry—dressed annually with 3 cwts. of potash to the acre, in addition to other manures, which did not accumulate enough potash to make satisfactory growth until its eighth year, after which it grew away well. In this instance the soil was a shallow, hot gravel over clay and notoriously potash-deficient.

The symptoms of potash shortage—and these should be recognised by many of my readers—are lack of growth, small leaf and leaves from which the glossy green dries out until a scorched margin surrounds the leaf. As a result the leaves cannot do their work properly, growth is reduced to a minimum and leaf falls early. Badly affected bushes remain like the four-year-old bush illustrated in Chapter III. on page 35. Incidentally that particular bush, which was drawn from life, came from a potash-deficient, sandy soil.

Lack of potash, however, must not always be blamed for poor growth. A very usual reason for young bushes failing to grow well is the insistence of the half-day jobbing gardener on tidying up weeds by digging them in. While admirable in the open ground close digging spells ruination to newly planted fruit bushes which are yearning for a firm root hold. So, when your gardener assures you that "Digging round 'em does 'em good," set him a job reclaiming or double-digging a piece of waste ground where his complexes can be released without damage, and take over the gooseberry patch yourself. The rooting system of the gooseberry is normally very widespread as well as deep, and any cultivation beneath the spread of its branches should be limited to hoeing. One should avoid planting vegetables among gooseberries if only for this cultural reason.

Manuring.

We have already mentioned the insistence of the gooseberry on adequate supplies of potash. Sulphate of potash, even at a modest ounce to the square yard, which is an average dressing, is unobtainable for fruit under wartime restrictions. To replace it we must turn to the bonfire ashes, and since their potash compounds are of the soluble type we should spread them around as soon as cool, thus avoiding heavy loss by rain. Moderate dressings of farmyard manure, which, if of good quality, may contain approximately 12 lb. of nitrogen, 12 lb. of potash and 6 lb. of phosphoric acid per ton, in addition to humus and all sorts of trace elements, will also serve to maintain the potash content of the soil. If this cannot be got hold of the garden compost heap must be called upon and provided Sir Albert Howard is not looking can be profitably reinforced by light dressings of a well-balanced manure such as Peruvian Guano. (Note: Not all Peruvian Guano comes from Peru, nor is it all Guano, so buy from a good source of supply). Quick-acting nitrogenous fertilisers are best avoided, since they induce lush growth which is very liable to go down to gooseberry mildew, about which you will hear later on. Where potash is known to be short, as indicated by the scorched edges to leaves, on no account try to force growth by nitrogen applications until the potash shortage has been remedied. It just cannot be done.

Raising Young Bushes.

When a one- or a two-year-old bush is planted the growth made in the past year or two years in the nursery is indicated by the season's wood, which is light to very light in colour. If there are two or four shoots these should be cut back to about three or four buds from their base, taking care to cut so that two side buds are left, thus doubling the number of shoots required to start the shape of the bush. Now let us see how a one-year-old bush is arrived at.

In raising gooseberry bushes on the "leg" as advised for the garden, stout, well-ripened shoots of the current season's wood, about 12 ins. long, are taken any time from October to December, but the earlier the better, and all the lower buds are removed, leaving only the top three or four. If buds on the lower section are left they will throw up shoots from below soil level and instead of a bush on a "leg" you will have a bush on a "stool." This, while making a larger and a more productive bush than the "leg" type, is hard to keep clear of perennial weeds, scutch grass and so forth, which, once they get a firm hold in the middle of the bush, cannot easily be "winkled out."

The best shoots for cuttings are usually pulled away with a "heel" from old, surplus branches which have been pruned out in an autumn thinning of a commercial plantation. Such shoots having torn away the thickened union at the base have a better "callus" development. Callus, in this case, is the sappy exudation which solidifies into a healing scar from around which new roots will spring.

The best soil in which to raise gooseberry cuttings is a gritty or a rich sandy loam, but any average soil which has raised a good crop of new potatoes will have enough manure left to ensure a good start. When enough cuttings have been prepared a line should be laid out and a spade slit made along it. On heavy land a sprinkle of sand along the slit will aid in rooting. Cuttings are then pushed down into the slit at 6-in. intervals, keeping the top buds well above soil level. The soil on both sides of the cutting row is then well firmed with a wooden rammer and a cultivator run both sides of the row.

Natural rooting also occurs and it is common when clearing up gooseberry bushes in winter, especially where drooping varieties are grown, to find that where a part of the shoot, or a growing tip, has made contact with the soil rooting has been effected. While these will make "stool" bushes they cannot be induced to form a "leg" and will always throw up sucker shoots. Such drooping types should have their leading shoots pruned to an upright bud in order to offset their drooping habit.

Pruning.

Under "Raising Young Bushes" we have demonstrated in the very first paragraph the preliminary steps to take in forming a bush. There are two schools of thought regarding the pruning of the adult or—shall we say—the gooseberry bush over four years of age. One holds that a framework of more or less permanent branches should be built up and maintained by annual tipping of the main extension growths and spurring in side growths to three or four buds, thus providing a rigid branch round which the fruit clusters closely. The ultimate shape of such a bush complete with leg resembles a short-handled umbrella.

In this type of pruning strong annual growths springing up in the centre of the bush are mainly discouraged, only a small proportion being retained to replace or supplement the main framework.

The other school of thought prefers to encourage the formation of strong, young shoots, which spring up and incline outwards as the weight of cropping exerts its pull, and to dispense with the spur-pruning of the main branches. These latter are kept well thinned out so that picking can be done in reasonable comfort. The two systems are equally sound provided that the spur-pruning is confined to the umbrella on a "leg" type, and the long shoot and thinning system is applied to the "stool" type.

The cordon gooseberry is as useful as the currant cordon and very large, easily-picked fruits can be had. (Plate VII). Raise cuttings as recommended for cordon currants ànd plant on walls or in the open as preferred.

Varieties to Grow.

Twenty years ago it was held by commercial growers that if the cherry crop was a failure it paid to hold gooseberries for ripening. Markets then had a regular seasonal demand for ripe berries. Those favoured were Whinham's Industry, Lancashire Lad and Warrington (three red varieties) and Yellow Rough.

In 1935 Mr. Rawes of the Royal Horticultural Society gave Warrington (red), Langley Gage (green), and Golden Drop as the three best dessert varieties for sheer quality, but for average garden requirements he thought that Whinham's Industry and Lancer (green), Leveller (yellow) and Whitesmith (white), would suffice.

In *Fruit Growing* (1935), Mr. Bagenal of East Malling Research Station describes Lancashire Lad as probably the best all-round berry for the market garden. Warrington as much esteemed for preserving, and Yellow Rough or, as it is called to-day, Early Sulphur, as of excellent flavour. Since then on the radio the late Mr. Middleton has advised Careless (green) and Leveller (yellow) as his choice.

Granted a casting vote I should suggest that the four best varieties for the garden would be Whinham's, Warrington, Leveller and Whitesmith.

All these latter, except Leveller, will stand sulphur spraying or dusting against mildew infection. Langley Gage, which Mr. Rawes chooses for a green berry, will not stand sulphur, nòr will Golden Drop, which is rather an important point in making a choice.

' To sum up the varieties mentioned, and there are many other choices, we have:

Careless: very large, milky green, and very good flavour. Drooping growth. For mid-season use green, but ripens early. Should not be grown beneath trees.

Early Sulphur: Medium size, golden yellow, good flavour.
Yellow Rough: Upright spreading grower. For early dessert.
Golden Drop: Small, greenish yellow, flavour good. Growth upright and sturdy. Mid-season.
Lancashire Lad: Large, ripens to red, when quality is fair. Good when cooked green. Makes a moderate-sized, upright, spreading bush. Mid-season.
Lancer: Medium size, colour green, excellent flavour. Growth strong and makes a large bush. Season late. (Mr. E. A. Bunyard classes this as "the best all-round green variety and perhaps the best of any colour.")
Langley Gage: Medium size, pale yellow-green, very good flavour. Strong, upright growth. Mid-season."
Leveller: Large, yellow-green, very good flavour. Growth fairly vigorous and spreading. Late season.
Warrington: Medium, pale red, flavour good. Vigorous but drooping habit of growth. Season late.
Whinham's Industry: Medium to large, dark red, flavour very good. Vigorous growth, making a large bush. Mid-season (Plate VII).
Whitesmith: Medium to large, very pale greenish-yellow, very good flavour. Growth vigorous, upright and later spreading. Mid-season.
Except for the richer and more sugar-sweet flavour of the best of the yellow varieties there is, in my opinion, little to choose between ripe gooseberries of recognised quality. The green gooseberry, picked for bottling while really small, provides a berry with a delicate, musky flavour which is unique. When full-grown this is completely lacking though the fruit is well enough cooked or jammed. When fully ripe its value as dessert depends to some extent on what else happens to be available but should make no demands on our sugar ration. Gooseberries should not be picked and kept but should be eaten or cooked as soon as convenient to avoid loss of flavour. A few elderberry blossoms enhance the muscatel flavour of young green gooseberries when stewed. A good succession of varieties helps to prolong their season.
Having mentioned ten of the best I do not propose to describe more varieties since to do so is rather reminiscent of the classic description of beers: "All beer is good but some beers are better than others," and to most gardeners a good

* Varieties so marked will not stand Lime-Sulphur Spraying.

cropper of fair quality is better than an indifferent cropper of superior quality.

Birds.

Birds can be perfect demons where gooseberry buds are concerned, stripping out the buds during winter and spring till too few are left to build up a young bush, let alone carry a crop of berries. Ripe fruit is, of course, fair game. The only satisfactory way to prevent small birds from pecking out the buds in their natural search for Vitamin C is to wind black cotton freely in and out and around the branches directly they have been pruned in early winter. Birds hate to have their toes tangled in these invisible strands and the sparrow or tom-tit which meets a cotton strand when in full flight must get a shock similar to that suffered by a Heinkel in unexpected contact with a barrage balloon cable.

Some slight relief can be expected where pruning is left until late in spring, provided the bushes are really dense. Tar Oil spraying also deters them, but must be completed in winter before growth starts. It also kills off a few troublesome weeds around the base, including chickweed.

Other Troubles of the Gooseberry.

The commonest insect pest attacking the gooseberry is the Gooseberry Sawfly caterpillar. Usually the presence of these pests is not noted until one or more of the bushes has been almost completely defoliated, apparently in a single night. Closer inspection shows the whole bush alive with the blue-green, black-spotted varmints. Actually the damage has taken two or three weeks to develop. The caterpillars hatch from eggs laid on the leaves during the blossoming period. Hardly noticeable at first, the tiny caterpillars soon develop and, feeding in the centre of the bush, or stripping a single branch, spread ever upwards and outwards until the leaf is completely cleared. The remedy is a simple one and if put on at the proper time to await the hatch of the eggs the threat of early damage can be forgotten, since the first meal will poison the lot. If preventive treatment is not taken and caterpillars are allowed to develop, then a non-poisonous Derris wash must be used as soon as live caterpillars are seen. The fly provides three generations in a season, the first in April and May, the second in June and the last in August. Derris will settle any attack if applied in time, and has the advantage of being non-poisonous.

If Arsenate of Lead Powder is made up as a wash the dose of $\frac{1}{4}$ lb. to 12 gallons of water will be strong enough. If Arsenate of Lead Paste is used, twice the weight of paste is needed. Derris being controlled by the Government, as a delousing agent, ready mixed proprietary wet sprays of this material are likely to be on sale for only a short time. When using these follow the makers' instructions.

It may be worth mentioning that the gooseberry sawfly caterpillars are very nervous creatures—oh yes, even our modern caterpillars have their weaknesses—and a simple method of ascertaining if they are about in force is to give the stem or a main branch of the bush a sharp tap with a walking stick. If present, most of them will fall to the ground, feigning death until such time as it is safe to go aloft again.

The currant clearwing moth caterpillar, which also attacks currants, occasionally damages the gooseberry, tunnelling up the interior of young, pithy shoots. There is no cure for this insect save the hunting out and destroying of individual specimens as and when discovered. When, at pruning time, a branch is seen to be hollow and blackened in the centre it may be removed and explored with a pair of secateurs till the intruder is found. If the branch, as sometimes happens, is a main leader the removal may spoil the bush unless a young growth can be trained in to replace it.

The magpie or currant moth, whose black-and-white caterpillars develop in August, sometimes attacks the leaf and these can then be dealt with by a Derris wash, as in the case of the late hatch of sawfly caterpillars, it being then too late for the use of Arsenate of Lead unless the gooseberry crop has been cleared green.

Other caterpillars may make their appearance, some of the usual apple-eating varieties, such as the winter moths and mottled umber moth, fancying an occasional change in diet. With arsenical washes and Derris, as wash or a dust, the gardener should be well able to deal with all and sundry— provided that he sees the enemy in time.

Greenfly can be an annoying pest even on the gooseberry, stunting the tip growth and twisting it out of shape. This damage is done in early summer, after which the greenfly leave for other host plants, returning in the autumn to lay their over-wintering eggs. The preventive remedy is to include the gooseberries in the Tar-oil winter washing of apples, plums and black currants, using a 5 per cent concentration (i.e. 2 qts. of Tar-oil to 10 gallons of water) between December and the end of February. This wash will also clear up any red spider of the type which is peculiar to the gooseberry, but, since these often develop elsewhere and come along to infest the bushes, if an attack develops in late spring the only safe remedy to apply (since sulphur is taboo to so many varieties of berry) is a 2 per cent White Oil Emulsion spray at the end of the flowering period and again a week later. The red spider, like the greenfly, is a sap-sucker and weakens the plant by its insatiable appetite.

Fungus Troubles.

American gooseberry mildew is the Brave New World's gift to the gooseberry grower and one which he could very well have done without. If you examine your gooseberry bushes in winter the odds are that you will find that the tips of some, many, or all of their new shoots are browned over. This indicates the over-wintering stage of the fungus and such tips should always be removed and burned. In summer the disease attacks the leaf to some extent, and the berry very visibly, as a white, felty patch. Soon the white turns to brown and a very unappetising little berry results. Various conditions tend to encourage the arrival and development of this trouble. Varieties are themselves inherently susceptible.[1]

[1] Among the more susceptible varieties are Lancer, Keepsake and Whinham's Industry, but, since these will stand Lime-sulphur wash and Sulphur dusting, a means of control is available. When, however, certain varieties such as most of the Yellows—Leveller, Yellow Rough and Golden Drop—are concerned and sulphur in any form causes serious loss of leaf and fruit, a different application must be made. This should consist of 4 lb. of washing soda, 1 lb. of soft soap (about a year's ration, I fear!) in 20 gallons of water. This spray is of no lasting effect since it is very easily washed off by rain. Once the mildew is noticed it must be sprayed with this wash and repetitions must be made, as spells of bad weather determine in order to maintain a cover. Where Lime-sulphur can be used the spray, at a concentration of 3 per cent, should go on as a routine spray before flowering (first week in April) and again at a concentration of no more than 1 per cent during the last week of April. Further applications at 1 per cent, or sulphur dustings, can be used if the summer be unduly wet and the mildew definitely troublesome, but if used on fruit, marking is unavoidable.

Other conditions predisposing to attack are: over-vigorous growth resulting from stimulation by too much nitrogenous manure, thus reducing resistance to disease; overcrowding by planting too close, or under trees, or allowing the bushes to get too dense, all of which conditions tend to prevent sun and free air movement. Sites which lie damp and where undue humidity of the air in summer exists are especially prone to attack.

Botrytis or Die-Back.

This is a fungus which battens on the dead. Where main branches, or even whole bushes, wilt and die, suspect this disease. Where the bush is grown on a leg complete destruction may ensue, but where the bush is grown as a stool only the affected branch will die ·to soil level. Both Whinham's Industry and Keepsake seem to be very liable to infection, but this fact should not trouble you unduly since the disease prospers only where left to its own devices. The remedy is to amputate the affected branch well below the wilted shoots and leaves just as soon as these are noticed in summer. Dead branches noticed in the spring should be removed and since the disease will spread on almost any decaying tissue from cabbages to cherries and raspberries to apples, general hygiene in the garden becomes of obvious importance.

There is a much more uncommon and interesting disease which attacks gooseberries growing near sedges, and which may be considered as a very local trouble. It is a fungus disease called cluster cup rust, which is a very adequate description. Since the trouble comes from the sedges their removal is all that is needed.

Fruit Splitting.

Gooseberries, like cherries, are apt to split in wet seasons. It often occurs to those varieties which grow large, e.g. Careless and Leveller. It is due to the berry almost finishing its growth under dryish conditions and then when the rain comes absorbing more water than its skin can accommodate.

X

GRAPES OUT OF DOORS

IF we were not, in the main, a nation at the mercy of money grubbers who much prefer buying imported foodstuffs to sell and re-sell again instead of allowing us to produce them for ourselves, it is quite certain that, instead of seeing indifferent German hocks on offer at £2 a bottle in this the third year of the war, we should be enjoying a better drink at a few shillings a bottle and keeping our money in the country. Excellent wine has been made from English grapes in the past, and there is no reason why it should not be made to-day if we cared to grow the grapes.[1] A Roman emperor, at the time of Britain's occupation by that race, even went so far as to say that he preferred the British wines to those of Gaul, a clear indication that in those days Imperial gullets were developed in preference to chins.

Gloucestershire and Worcestershire were great grape-growing counties in the days of the monasteries. In *A History of Worcestershire Agriculture*, by R. C. Gant, the author states that Bede, who died in A.D. 735, "mentioned vines in sundry places in England prior to 731. In 1086 there were 38 vine-yards in the vicinity of Evesham," while in the twelfth century grapes from the vines in Gloucestershire " were more pleasant in flavour than any in England." Bredon Hill was one of the Worcestershire sites and the light calcareous soil, in some places little more than broken oolitic limestone rock, should be ideal for grape growing. The Eastern and South-Eastern counties, too, knew all about grape growing. The monasteries were the great wine-makers and when they were disbanded the vineyards perished. In 1875 a vineyard was planted for Lord Bute at Castell Coch in Glamorganshire. It was extended by cuttings taken and grown in the same way as are currant cuttings, the vines making good strong plants within two years. Mr. Andrew Pettigrew, who was respon-sible for the planting of the vineyard, says in *The Fruit Garden* (Country Life Library, 1904): "The vintage of 1881 was

[1] A Suffolk fruit-grower who planted vines in a field writes: "I tried and failed. The soil was wrong, it should be light, and I got too much growth. I am sure that in East Anglia or East Kent it can be done, given light soil, lying high, facing south or west."

excellent in quality, and the whole of it was sold (except for a few dozen) at 60/- a dozen to a wine merchant in Cardiff. Dr. Lawson Tait, late of Birmingham, a noted connoisseur in wines, bought several dozens of it from the wine merchant in question, some of which was sold by auction at Birmingham the following year and realized 115/- a dozen." The grape grown at Castell Coch is mentioned as Gamay Noir, a hardy variety of Northern France. These vineyards became derelict and were grubbed during the First World War.

These outdoor vines for wine production are severely pruned and are quite unlike the grape vines which one occasionally sees clustering on the walls of houses in London and elsewhere. Good quality grapes for dessert can be easily grown on a warm south or south-east wall which gets plenty of sun and the size of grape produced is determined mainly by the methods of pruning, training and treatment (Plate VIII).

If a vine planted against a wall makes a good start its roots will very soon extend far in all directions. It is usually stated in gardening books that a light or friable, warm, well-drained soil is essential, but experience shows that a strong, holding soil may prove better in the long run provided that a good start is given by seeing that drainage below the root is good and that ample supplies of lime, preferably of the old mortar type, are available. When planting the vine a few shovelsful of bonfire ashes and burnt earth and a handful of raw bone of coarse grade will be valuable, but need only be given where soil is poor.

Some interesting details were broadcast early in February 1945 concerning the famous vines of Kippen in Stirlingshire. In this spot grows the largest vine in the world (America please note and be duly humble). Four other vines there are the largest in Great Britain. Buchanan More of Kippen planted this famous vine in 1891, out of a small pot. By 1922 it had attained world's champion dimensions. From tip to tip it measures 300 ft. Its main stem has a girth of 46 ins., and in 1940 it yielded 3,000 bunches. It is interesting to note that the famous vine at Hampton Court is now 170 years old, and though regarded by many as the largest in the country must take a back seat to all the Kippen clan.

Planting.

October is a good month in which to plant, but if that month be missed, February, or in a late season, March, will

VINE TRAINED HORIZONTALLY.
The small black squares indicate the buds left to carry fruit. The breaks in the line of the shoots indicate where buds have been removed.

do. Cuttings taken in October and heeled in through the winter will root readily in their permanent quarters if planted in February. If you have bought your vine in a pot, turn it out and spread out the roots, setting it about a foot from the wall, 6 ins. deep and firming the soil around it thoroughly. Manure or mulching is unnecessary. Only if conditions become very dry need very diluted manure water be given.

Vines can be grown on walls as cordons, or straight rods, set out at 3 ft. or 4 ft. apart; they can be trained around a door or a window or trained as a many-branched wall pear. When grown as a cordon each vine is trained up as a single stem, allowing side shoots to develop at 15-in. to 18-in. intervals, which shoots are cut hard back each autumn or winter to a single eye or bud. Where a single vine is grown to cover a large wall space it should be trained on the same lines as a horizontally-trained wall pear. To do this the young plant is beheaded above a bud, at about 18 ins. from soil level, after planting. The three top buds will break, growing into shoots. The two lower shoots are trained left and right horizontally, the top shoot is trained vertically. After a season's growth the central upright shoot is again cut back to about half its growth or less. The horizontal shoots are treated similarly. Both vertical shoot and horizontal shoots will, during the ensuing season, produce side shoots; some of these are wanted, some are not. On the vertical centre shoot the only shoots needed are those intended to form horizontal branches. On the horizontal branches all shoots on the lower side of the branch should be rubbed off and those on the upper side should be limited to about a foot apart. From these fruit will eventually come.

Extension, if the vine is growing well, should average about 3 ft. to 4 ft. a year after pruning has been done, and at this rate a fair-sized wall can soon be covered. Once the allotted space has been filled the extension growth is stopped by repeated pinching off and the only other pruning needed is the close spurring in of all lateral shoots.

Disbudding.

Once the main shape of the vine is achieved the side shoots will produce buds which will develop into laterals or secondary side shoots. These are only wanted for fruiting purposes and so must be limited so that they are spaced no closer than a foot apart and all emanating from the upper side of the main shoots. When about 5 ins. or 6 ins. long a strong lateral (or side growth) will show a flower cluster, springing from its base with several leaves above it and a growing tip. If this shoot is to be allowed to bear fruit the tip should be pinched off, leaving two leaves above the flower cluster. This pinching off is the only operation needed during the growing season save for the rubbing out of unwanted buds.

Cropping.

A vine should never be allowed to over-crop during its early years, as the resultant check to growth will affect cropping for several years. One bunch at the third season and five in the fourth is enough. After that the strength of the vine should decide the weight of crop to be allowed. Roughly, when a vine measures 2 ins. round the stem below its first horizontal branch it should be fit to carry 5 lb. of fruit, and for every $\frac{1}{2}$ in. added another 5 lb. may be allowed.

Once in regular fruiting apply liquid manure and a mulch

during the growing season, spreading both well away from the stem since the roots are by then extensive and widespread.

Thinning is the most tedious operation in vine culture but when done out of doors is a picnic compared to indoor thinning. It is essential to thin if one requires sizeable fruit. The aim should be to leave the centre of the cluster clear of fruitlets, with the grapes which are left spaced evenly around the outside. In the case of very large bunches under glass the thinners will support side shoots of the fruit cluster with a raffia tie to give the grapes more room in which to develop, but this is rarely necessary in outdoor culture.

Thinning can be begun as soon as the grapes are big enough to handle, using a pair of scissors with pointed ends. About one or two fruits should be removed to each one left.

Varieties.

Black Hamburgh: This is a well-known cold-house variety and is one of the best black grapes to grow outside. The famous Hampton Court vine is of this variety. If well grown it can be large and luscious, but it is rather liable to mildew.

Royal Muscadine: Is the best outdoor white grape. Its fruit, which is amber in colour and not white, is sweet and good, and it is as hardy as Black Hamburgh.

Black Judy and *Black Prince* are also good varieties for warm walls if the two first-named are not obtainable.

Since the first edition of this book was issued more information on grape growing out of doors has come my way. In the December 1943 issue of the Royal Horticultural Society's Journal, Mr. James Wingfield published an article describing his own experiences with this fruit. He has kindly given me the following details.

VARIETIES.

On the outskirts of London he has grown and cropped out of doors the following: *Black Grapes:* Brandt, Gamay Frew, Black Hamburgh. *White Grapes:* Royal Muscadine and Muscatel.

Propagation.

All the above are easily raised from cuttings. To do this a well-ripened shoot is taken and a clean cut made outwards with a sharp knife from behind an eye or bud. This

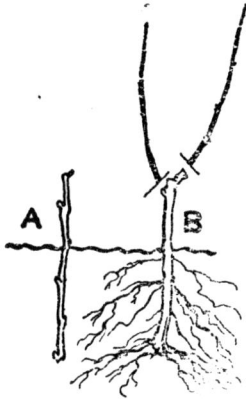

should be done in October. The cuttings can be up to 16 ins. long and the number of buds they have is immaterial. Bundles of up to twelve cuttings are planted in a sheltered corner in ordinary un-manured soil about a foot deep and if the weather is cold can be protected with some litter. Here they remain till spring. Then in February the bundle is lifted and the cuttings are planted out in the place where they are to remain.

A shows a vine cutting planted for rooting.
B the cutting in its second year after pruning.

Training.

Vines must be pruned extremely hard—as hard indeed as the mis-guided amateur is apt to prune his apple trees (see *Tree Fruit Growing*, Vol I., Plate XI). The rooted cutting will throw out shoots from every bud above ground and all these will be cut hard back to a single or at most two buds at the end of each autumn for the first three years. The seasonal

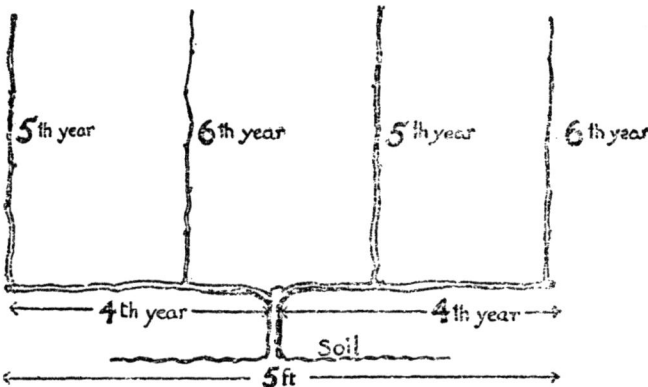

VINE TRAINED VERTICALLY. The stem is formed in the first three prunings. In the fourth year two horizontal shoots are trained. Vertical shoots are trained in 5th and 6th years.

shoot growths made can be loosely tied up to a post during
the growing period. This drastic pruning is simply to build
up a good stem and root system for future performance.
At the end of the third season only three eyes are left on the
short stem and one of these is simply left in case of accidental
loss of one of the remaining two.

During the fourth year the three buds are allowed to develop
two shoots which are trained out horizontally and in autumn
are cut back to about 2 ft. 6 ins. in length, choosing a bud
which is upright.

In the fifth year each horizontal is allowed to grow a vertical
shoot and in the sixth year another vertical shoot is allowed
to each. This gives a four-shooted gridiron shape about
5 ft. across. The vertical shoots are headed back and stopped
when they reach their allotted height, which may be on a wall,
a fence or a trellis. For wider covering more vertical shoots
can be encouraged.

Cropping.

No more than 5 bunches are allowed on each 5th-year shoot
during the 5th season. After that each two shoots will come
into fruiting during the season.

Manuring.

Grapes apparently need no manure at all during their lives.
They are perfectly happy in sand and broken stone provided
there is enough moisture for their wide-rooting system. One
can blow up grapes with manure, increase the size of
individual fruits and bunches, but only at a loss of flavour and
sweetness. Hard pruning is the secret of success, and though
a vine will gladly cover a whole house-side in a few years'
time, to produce grapes it had far better be cut to the semblance
of an Irishman's shillelagh than allowed to ramble at will.

Pests and Diseases.

Red spider is a pest which always attacks wall fruit trees
where proper attention is not given to watering in dry weather.
This state of affairs is always common to wall fruits unless
the owner realises that a tree against a wall is normally deprived
of much rain, and that further droughting of the already dry
area sheltered by the wall is caused by the porous nature of

the wall itself, which is forever absorbing moisture and losing it again to the air in hot sun or wind.

To combat spider enough water at the root should be the first step and regular syringing of the leaves from beneath in fine evenings should be the second. If these have been neglected and an attack has already developed then a Derris spray is the best to give, following the makers' directions as to mixing.

The peeling off, during winter, of all the old, loose bark from vine stems and branches will be found to reduce pests almost to vanishing point.

Powdery Mildew.

This disease is very common on grapes both indoor and outdoor. As the name suggests, white patches of mildew appear on leaves, fruit and shoots. When the fruit is attacked many of the grapes will fall and others will crack and go rotten. Mildew can be prevented by allowing a generous spacing of the fruiting shoots and by frequent dusting with sulphur dust or spraying with soluble sulphur during the growing season.

XI

THE RASPBERRY

WILD raspberries are met with in many places in England, but they are seldom of any value, fruits being small and inclined to dryness. When sizeable fruits are found growing wild they are usually relics from the garden of a cottage which has long since disappeared, or they are chance seedlings from cultivated varieties spread by birds. Many years ago the writer noticed a field of Baumforth raspberries at one end of which a dozen rows of an autumn-fruiting variety—November Abundance—had been planted on the off-chance of their being a useful addition to the fruit crop. The Baumforths were picked regularly; the latter, being of little commercial value and coming at an awkward time, remained unpicked and were enjoyed by the birds. A few years after planting, such a forest of November Abundance canes had sprung up among the Baumforth rows as the result of birds flying off with the fruit to eat at leisure that the whole piece of raspberries became unprofitable and was grubbed and burnt. This particular variety, apparently, comes true, or nearly true, from seed.

To-day, the varieties which are considered commercially profitable can be numbered on one hand, but this does not by any means include the total number which are available. It is an interesting fact that of the varieties listed in catalogues of a hundred years ago very few are to be found to-day.

As with the strawberry, virus disease has played havoc with most strains of raspberry during the past decade. It is not easy to find an explanation as to why this has come about; whether it is due to the gradual change over in manuring from farmyard manure to inorganic artificials resulting in a lowering of the plant's resistance to disease, or to the introduction of less resistant strains of new varieties, or to the uncontrolled distribution of stock from centres known to be infected with virus trouble,[1] is a problem for the research worker. There is no doubt that much of it dates from the reckless distribution in the early twenties when any cane could be sold at a profit and you could please yourself what name you gave

[1] In pre-war days about a million canes a year were dug from plantations in the affected areas of Scotland and sent South to be sold, for the most part, to amateurs.

it. Whatever the reason for the decline of a variety the only
remedy would seem to be to start with sound stock and uproot
and destroy any weak or diseased cane at sight, thus building
up a surviving strain which is resistant.

Soil.

Being a very fibrous-rooted plant the raspberry is at its
best in a rich medium-heavy soil, and, on land which suits
it, may remain profitable for as long as ten or even twenty
years. It likes plenty of moisture but resents waterlogging,
and a blocked drain across a raspberry field is usually shown
by a line of dead canes. Provided it is planted in heavily
manured and deeply dug soil it will need no other type of
manuring than farmyard. Where this cannot be had compost
should be made and used, and only organic manures such as
fish meal, meat meal, dried blood and bone meal should be
given. Occasionally, on soils which are unduly deficient in
potash (sands, hot gravels, and so forth), scorched edges to
the leaves indicate the shortage and steps should be taken to
replace the deficiency by adding a little sulphate of potash
or diverting some of the ashes from bonfires to the raspberry
rows. No artificial manure should ever be sown on the
crowns of the canes, but should go on the sides of the rows.

Selecting Stock.

Raspberries for planting should not really be drawn from the
fruiting rows unless you are sure that the strain is strong and
healthy. Many hundreds of thousands of canes have been so
drawn every season, quite regardless of their condition.

The proper way to raise raspberry canes for distribution
is to plant sound canes in rows 6 ft. apart with the canes at
18 ins. to 2 ft. apart in the row. The canes are cut down to
6 ins. at planting time and at the end of the growing season
are either cut down again (to make sure there is no fruiting
wood) or the whole of the canes which have come up are dug
out, leaving nothing but the fibrous roots in the soil. The canes
can then be graded for quality. Next year many more canes
will come up and all these again can be dug. It is estimated
that a plant of 300 canes will yield up to 4,000 or more by the
third season.

Just how much cane is thrown up depends on the variety,
for example, Newburgh is a very free spawning cane while
Pyne's Imperial is comparatively sparse in its response. Lloyd
George also is very free compared to Norfolk Giant.

When raised in this' way from supposedly clean stock the nurseryman will still have to rogue his stock twice a year in the summer and grub out any odd or suspicious looking types. If he is wise he will not omit a fungicidal spray of Bouisol at prescribed strength or Bordeaux Mixture (4 x 6 x 100), or Lime Sulphur as recommended under the heading Cane Spot in the section dealing with diseases.

If you decide to buy raspberry canes from any particular source, trusted or otherwise, either go and see the canes in the summer or ask and if needs be pay for a good average sample. Before you do this write to H.M. Stationery Office, York House, Kingsway, London, W.C.2, and enclose a penny stamp asking for a copy of Ministry of Agriculture Leaflet No. 77, Raspberry Diseases in Scotland. In that you will find various raspberry diseases illustrated, including Spur Blight. This is a fungus centred around the buds and showing as a purple patch often extending right round the cane. With the leaflet in your hand you will have no difficulty in identifying it if your sample suffers from the disease. Also look for a much more serious disease, Cane Blight, which can kill the cane at or above soil level by destroying the bark. This is indicated in winter by cracked brown and broken bark around the base of the cane with the thin bark covering peeling off. If examined carefully you will find scattered about in the dead sections clusters of little round black dots. These are the fruiting stage of the fungus. Such canes should be avoided at all costs and nothing planted but slick clean canes.

Varieties.

In 1826 the gardener visiting the Horticultural Society's garden at Chiswick could see twenty-three varieties of raspberry growing well. In 1872 he could have bought from at least one good old nursery firm in Somerset some fourteen varieties of which no more than three (Semper Fidelis and perhaps a Red and Yellow Antwerp) could be found in any English garden of to-day.

In *The Cultivation of Berried Fruits in Great Britain*, published 1946 by Crosby Lockwood and Co., London, the author, Mr. Charles H. Oldham, quotes a list of raspberries taken from an article by Mr. N. H. Grubb in 1922, which describes the characteristics of some thirty-five varieties and variants.

Considering the comprehensive nature of this book it seems a little strange that a list of varieties described in 1922 should

Plate I Though strawberries and raspberries like some shade, note the effect on brussels sprout plants of planting near a beech row. It is useless to expect soft fruits to flourish in soil which is robbed by large trees or old hedgerows.

Plate II Merton Thornless Blackberry. Two-thirds natural size. A nice example of the controlled scientific development of a better fruit than the original parents.

East Malling Research Station

Plate III Reversion of Black Currant: Fully reverted
branch on left. Note nettle leaf effect and
absence of fruits. Sound branch on right with
normal leaves and carrying good fruits.

Plate IV

A branch of Hilltop Baldwin Black Currant, exactly as cut off, i.e., no leaves removed and no fruits added. Though a weak grower on some soils, it crops enormously where well looked after.

Plate V

Big-bud Mite of Black Currants. The mite (inset) is approximately 600 times life size. Within this microscopic creature lives the ultra-microscopic virus infection of Reversion. Both the twigs carry ' big buds,' and the growth at each tip indicates a condition of full Reversion.

Dr. A. M. Massee

Plate VI   Red Currant: Wilson's Long Bunch four years planted.

Plate VII A treble cordon-trained gooseberry of
the variety Whinham's Industry. Training is easy and very fine fruits result.

Plate VIII A productive grape vine on a stone wall.

Plate IX The Newburgh raspberry in fruit.
This is an American variety still
hardly known in England. Fruit is
large, very bright red colour, but seeds
are rather bigger than other kinds.

(With acknowledgments to the Editors of *The Journal of Pomology*).

Plate X Two forms of Raspberry Mosaic disease, not to be confused with Chlorosis (a general yellowing of the leaf). Note the irregular blotching on the leaf and downward curl, both characteristic of this virus disease.

Plate XI Royal Sovereigns in Devonshire. First year of fruiting. Apparently sound and healthy.

Plate XII A year later, looking up the field. The
virus disease 'Crinkle' has wiped out
all the plants in the foreground.

Plate XIII A double row of Baron Solemacher
Alpine Strawberries. This variety
produces no runners, and is easily
(when seed is procurable) grown
from seed.

Plate XIV A typical healthy truss of Royal Sovereign strawberries. About your two years' ration in wartime.

Plate XV Large scale composting. Old tomato stems and all manner of refuse from sixteen acres of glasshouses is rotted
down in permanent shallow pits. Note the loose tiles
which cover air ducts beneath the compost.

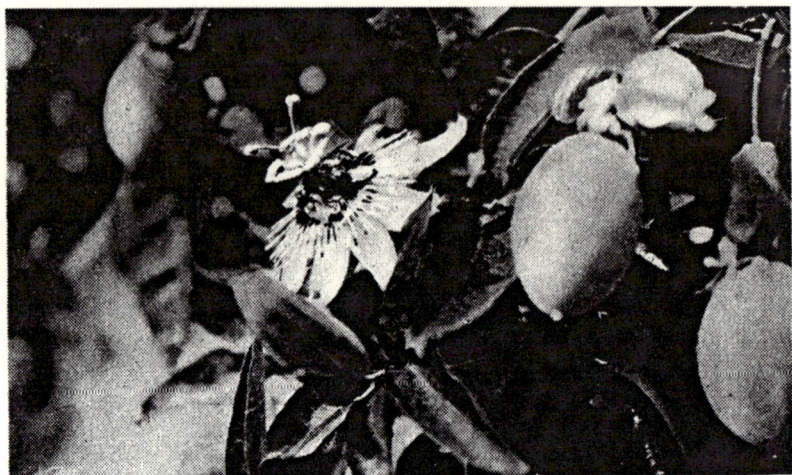

Plate XVI Passiflora Incarnata growing on a Surrey wall. Note the egg-shaped fruits and the flower centre clustered with sipping bees.

Plate XVII Outdoor Tomatoes grown in the Evesham manner.

Plate XVIII Outdoor Tomato. Stonor's M.P. Planted out against a wall on May 10th, 1943, and protected with Dutch lights (one of which is shown), cropped over 8 pounds per plant. No leaves have been removed.

Plate XIX Three Raspberry Beetles(greatly magnified)exploring a
blossom.   These are pale brown and about one-sixth
of an inch long.   The beetle lays her eggs in the
blossom, the hatched grub attacking the fruits.
Easily controlled by spraying.

be considered representative of 1946. Mr. Grubb is the authority on raspberry varieties and as an old friend I sent him the following list of raspberry varieties which I culled from catalogues printed during the last five years and asked for his candid comments. After all, unless one is candid on the subject of fruit varieties, it is no use writing about the subject at all. The catalogue can say what it fancies but the author should speak the truth.

List of possible Raspberry Varieties, all of which have been offered in nursery catalogues during the war years, 1939–46.

*Only varieties in heavy type can be generally recommended.

Bath's Perfection: It is most unlikely that this is correctly named. I have not seen a good stock of it for fifteen years.

Baumforth's Seedling: Probably Baumforth B. Very good dessert quality. Poor cropper. Very susceptible in Scotland to the leaf curl virus.

Brocket Hall: Never much good at East Malling. Said to be first class in Cornwall.

Brown's Seedilng: A new one to me.

Corfe Mullen Wonder: Never tried at East Malling. Not very impressive at Wisley.*

Deutschland: Not specially good at East Malling. when first tried. Went down with Mosaic much more quickly than Lloyd George.

Hailsham: Twenty-five years ago this was a passable autumn fruiter. Very doubtful if true to name.

Laxton's Alpha: Never outstanding at East Malling. Not impressive at Wisley.

Laxton's Reward: Used to be fair at East Malling, but not outstanding there or at Wisley.

Laxton's Autumn Giant: A new name to me.

Lloyd George: Must be mentioned in any list. Amos's and Plumpton strains are both fairly good, but not nearly so good as Lloyd George used to be. The New Zealand strain, now being propagated in isolation, is believed to be entirely virus free and may restore the variety, but this means waiting four or five years at least.

Matchless: One of the best of the newer varieties at East Malling. Grows and crops fairly well. Fruit is usually soft.

Newburgh: In some soils the fruit is too crumbly. No indication of virus. If we can control midge and cane blight it will be one of the best available raspberries.

* Wisley refers to the Royal Horticultural Society fruit trials.

D

Norfolk Giant: Must be mentioned in any list. Very late ripening. Poor dessert quality but cans and bottles very well. Many growers complain of poor cropping, but it has often reached three tons an acre at East Malling. Very susceptible in Scotland to leaf curl virus.

Park Lane: I never saw it cropping really well even twenty-five years ago. Many of the buds were blind and failed to grow. Best dessert quality. Very doubtful if now true to name.

Preussen: Good garden variety, not now planted commercially, as plants are usually short lived. Best of all in dessert quality but fruit often soft.

Pyne's Imperial and *Pyne's Royal:* Very similar. Very seldom make enough canes to crop decently but very good where they do. Most growers who still have them are planting other sorts.

Pyne's Red Cross: Probably wrongly named, unless in Pyne's own catalogue. So far as I know the true variety has gone clean out and is now unobtainable.

Reigate: According to Wisley this is indistinguishable from Lloyd George. May be healthier and more vigorous than the average Lloyd George.

St. Walfried: Fairly easy to obtain healthy and true to name. Goes down with virus more quickly than some. Moderate dessert quality at best but crops well. No good for canning.

Semper Fidelis: Which one? The varieties that used to be called Semper Fidelis have long ago died out except for the sixty-year-old row at Sherridge, near Malvern, so far as I know.

The Devon: Messrs. Chivers still grow it in Angus (Scotland) but no one else so far as I know. Very likely this is misnamed. The true Devon is very late.

YELLOW VARIETIES

Trinder's Golden Yellow: Not known to me.

Lord Lambourne: This is the only one of the three that I know. When first introduced it used to be the best of the Yellows, like a Yellow Lloyd George. I have not seen it for several years.

Yellow Magnum Bonum: Not known to me.

From the above list and Mr. Grubb's candid comments it will be seen that the choice of reliable raspberries is very limited and that the whole business of raspberry growing is in

a state of flux. I understand that some forty seedling rasp-
berry varieties are on trial and that already four of Mr.
Grubb's seedlings are being tried out on a big scale in many
districts and are giving good results. These are Malling Promise,
Malling Enterprise, Malling Landmark and Malling Notable.
Malling Promise has the largest fruit of any variety grown in
England. All these should be on sale in nurseries within the
next few years and may be something to look forward to.

In my own experience a variety which promised wonderfully
well was Lloyd George. It was only named after that great
man because, like him, it was liable to "raise cane" in no small
degree. He had nothing whatever to do with its production.
Although this variety has in many, indeed in most, cases degen-
erated in strength and stature, there are still strains in Kent
and in Essex which retain all the robustness of its early years.

In Scotland, in the areas where raspberries are grown on a
big scale for canning and preserving, the decline and fall of
one variety after another has been catastrophic. In the last
forty years Superlative, with its large fine fruit, has disappeared,
to be supplanted by Mitchell's Seedling, in turn to be deposed
by Baumforth's Seedling B—very popular in the 'twenties.
This also collapsed and was followed by Lloyd George, and now
with this fine variety on the wane many growers are extending
their acreage of Norfolk Giant. This is a useful berry, since
it is late enough in blooming to miss the frost. It remains
to be seen how long Norfolk Giant will stand up, but this
variety can at least be bought as certified by Government
inspection to be free of visible Mosaic disease.

There are at the moment a large number of seedling varieties
undergoing trial at testing stations. Some would appear to
be very good indeed, but it will be some time before much
can be said about them. There are also to be met with occasionally in private gardens, sound strains of some of the old
varieties which have gone out of commerce. For example,
in 1918 I gave a few dozen canes of Semper Fidelis which I
was then growing commercially to a friend and forgot all
about them. In 1935 I saw that the same canes were still
growing away well. Again in 1923 I planted an acre or two
of Pyne's Royal, then a newish, large-berried fruit which was
attractive for retail sale. I let a friend in Sussex have a hundred canes for his garden and when I visited him in 1944 he
happened to mention that the original plants were still in his
garden and cropping well. In my case within five years of

planting the whole lot had been grubbed and burned, owing to devastating attacks by the raspberry beetle, for in those days we had no Derris or D.D.T. with which to control the pest. Anxious to try again I begged a few canes from my friend to plant in my garden, where they failed miserably.

There is one point which large-scale research workers do not mention. Whereas acres go down to virus diseases, there are isolated patches in gardens which remain free of infection over long periods. Many such patches have lost vigour through bad management and many look sad and dwarfed with the yellow leaf of chlorosis induced by iron, magnesium or manganese deficiency, but they are not necessarily being attacked by virus disease.

My experience is that in a garden of really good soil, richly-manured with farmyard muck, raspberries can show mosaic on the leaf and still remain vigorous year after year. I have had seedling raspberries full of mosaic but able to throw canes ten feet high and keep on doing so. From this one may suppose that not all the decline of raspberry varieties must be credited to virus disease.

Planting.
Canes may be planted as late as April, but late autumn is the best time, since fat, white shoot buds are developing and these become overlong and brittle by spring and are apt to be broken off. Plant in rows 6 ft. apart for moderate growers and 7 ft. or even 8 ft. apart for the strong growers. Plants should be $1\frac{1}{2}$ ft. to 2 ft. apart in the row, according to the strength of the variety and its propensity for producing cane. The rooted canes should be buried to the earth mark on the cane and the soil well firmed above the roots. When winter is over the newly planted canes should be cut down to a bud about 8 ins. to 10 ins. above soil level. What buds are left will then produce an occasional fruit shoot and a few leaves, but, from the root, will arise one or more stout canes for cropping next season. To plant canes and expect heavy crops of fruit the same year (as lying press advertisements like to suggest) is foolish. A few berries will mature on the shoots emanating from the cut-down canes, but nothing worth having matures from unpruned canes, and the cane for next season is weakened, thus further postponing a crop.

Newly planted rows should be well mulched against spring drought with old rotted manure or compost or even lawn mowings, and, if the summer be unduly dry, watering is worth while.   Great care should be taken before planting to make sure that the soil is free of roots of perennial plants and, during the first year or two, to keep deep-rooting weeds such as scutch grass, buttercup, dandelion, dock and convolvulus from gaining a foothold in the rows, as later it will be impossible to get rid of them without damaging the raspberry canes.

 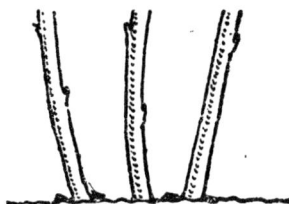

How not to prune   The right way

1st   2nd   3rd   and 4th prunings

Black portions indicate canes to be removed

Manuring.

Chlorosis is a deficiency trouble and arises from the inability of the plant to utilise iron in its tissues.   It is usually caused by too much lime in the soil.   Owing to the lack of iron the green is missing in the leaf sap or chlorophyll and the leaf, which is really the factory which works to make root and so growth, is put out of gear.   Yellow leaf and poor growth results.

One cannot be too insistent regarding the damage which may result from the indiscriminate use of lime among soft fruits.   It is seldom necessary or beneficial save in exceptional circumstances.

To grow the best soft fruits use plenty of animal manure or compost or organic manures such as meat and bone, dried

Supporting Raspberry canes without ties.

blood, hoof and so forth. Personally I am quite happy to see my soil surface green with mould in wet winters.

Pruning.

The raspberry sends out long exploring roots from which new shoots arise in addition to those centred around the original stool. Most growers chop off such unwanted suckers when hoeing the rows, leaving only the new canes which are in line with the original row. Once fruiting is over all those canes which have carried fruit can be cut down to soil level and carried out and burned. In late autumn all those canes which are surplus to the row—four being ample for a stool—are dug out, using a small spade and a gloved hand to pull with, in order to disturb the main roots as little as possible. In sandy soil canes may often be pulled without using a spade. Having taken out the surplus canes the rows are then ready for training.

Training.

With the coming of spring the tops of the canes (which are often unripened and partly dead) are cut back to pushing buds, or in the case of very tall growers (and 12 ft. has often been exceeded) are cut back to a height convenient for picking, 4 ft. to 5 ft. being sufficient. The effect of this cutting back is to concentrate growth in the reduced number of buds, giving finer fruit and, by reducing the shading of adjoining rows, allowing next season's canes to ripen up, thus lessening the

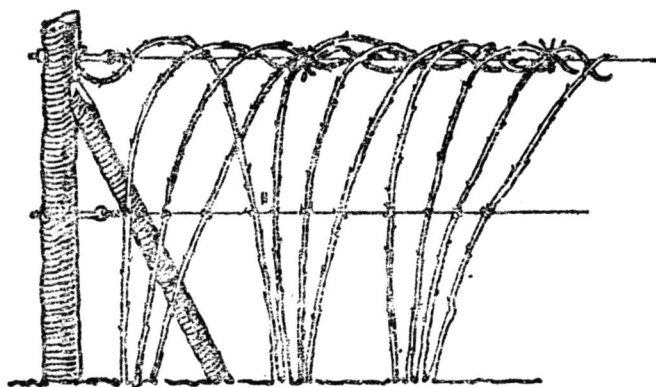

Overlapping Raspberry canes.

likelihood of fungus infections and improving the whole
condition of the raspberry patch.

There are several methods of supporting raspberries.
Where wires are used stout supports, well-strutted, so that a
tight wire can be secured are necessary. One or two double
rows of wires, secured by a wooden spreader at 12 in. apart
and set at 2 ft. and 4 ft. to 5 ft. apart according to the strength
of the canes, are a convenient method which obviates tying
in. A single wire can also be used and the canes held in
place by running a single length of binder twine in and out
among the canes and round the wire.

A very pretty method of training a variety like Norfolk
Giant which, when tall, is not brittle, is to strain two wires
between the posts, one at 3 ft. and the other at 4 ft. above
soil. Starting at the beginning of the row the canes are first
evenly spaced out and tied to the 3 ft. wire. The first cane is
then bent over and round the wire and secured in position
by bringing the next cane over and round it, this rope-making
being continued to the far end of the row, where the last
cane is securely tied. A few additional ties here and there
make for security and complete a very ship-shape job. Bending
the canes seems to increase the fruit production and the amount
which is condensed into a small space is astonishing.

I have tried all these methods but the system I prefer to use
is to strain two wires between posts at 3 ft. and 4 ft. from the
ground and to tie each cane in on both wires with soft string.

There is no point in growing the canes above the 4 ft. 6 in. mark and canes so tied in and reduced to that height are stiff and strong, carry better fruit and do not blow about. Where canes grow very strongly one cane per foot run is enough to grow. Hard cutting back of strong cane and plenty of room makes for very large fruit.

If no wires are the order of the day one can grow rasps around a central pole or the canes can be made to support each other by tying them in at threes about the half-way mark and not leaving them too tall.

Pruning for Autumn Raspberries.

There are, of course, autumn-fruiting raspberries, November Abundance being the best known, though in November its fruit having been seared by wind and frost and over-explored by fruit-minded flies is of little use and the raisers would have done better to have christened it October Abundance and left it at that. The Hailsham Berry is another, and if a true strain can still be had, is the best of the autumn-fruiting sorts. Indian Summer is said to be excellent but I know no nurseryman who raises it.

Autumn fruiting raspberries are, however, usually left to grow as summer varieties, thus failing to take advantage of their possibilities. The correct method is to cut all the canes produced in one year to within 4 in. or 5 in. of the soil in February, or a little later when winter is relaxing its grip. The new canes will then crop at their tips in their first year of growth instead of, as is the case in summer-fruiting varieties, growing a cane one year to produce fruit the year after.

Lloyd George, in autumn, normally carries a shoot here and there laden with magnificent berries. This is particularly noticeable in its first year after planting. Because of this habit it can be made into an autumn-fruiter where garden space allows. To do this, beginning with an established row which would normally fruit in July and August, cut away in June all the fruiting canes and allow the new young suckers to receive the impetus of growth which the last year's canes would have enjoyed.

Since autumn fruiting may be preceded by summer drought, if you would grow good fruit be prepared to supply water and dilute liquid manure to the canes when conditions indicate the need for it.

Cultivation.

It is common to see the fruit garden well and truly dug from end to end, and such reckless disregard of rooting systems argues little sympathy or understanding on the part of the digger. Cultivation among raspberries should always be very shallow near the rows. To dig up the centres of the alleys

between the rows is permissible and necessary, as one does not want a mat of rooting suckers to develop. Rotted manure or compost should be spread along the rows as a mulch and any available surplus should be spread between the rows. This can then be turned in with a spade, taking care to cut a shallow slit parallel with the rows and a foot from them so that a 2-ft. wide section, in which the plants are centred, remains undisturbed. Fresh foraging roots will soon work out from the rows and get busy, nor will their removal next winter be of any consequence.

From some photos of raspberry roots sent me from Australia, it seems that this plant can root in two ways. On deep, rich alluvial soil it may make a certain amount of fibrous root around soil level and four to five inches below, and a great mass of root going down to as much as five feet below the surface. On shallow soil or wet soil it may only have the upper root formation, and when this is the case the cane growth in a dry time will be poor and any deep cultivation between the rows will be very damaging. The deep-rooting plants, on the other hand, are more or less independent of the top soil rooting system and grow vigorously and bear heavily, whatever the season.

Picking.

Raspberries, if picked when well pink, will ripen to full colour and in this condition are not liable to bleed.   If they are to be sent away by rail (which Heaven forbid save in properly packed large scale consignments) or are picked for use the day following, they should be gathered in the cool of the morning, slightly on the under-ripe side.   Except in the case of extra fine fruit, cut off for dessert, the core or "plug" should be left on the stalk.   Until this stage of ripeness is reached the plug does not pull out readily.

Ripe raspberries will only keep a day or so under ordinary conditions of storage, though the modern "quick-freeze' method of dealing with fruit will give them a two-year life in cold storage.   In hot and thundery weather the juice soon begins to exude and mould will often appear overnight where commercial picking is in progress.   Where jam is the object the riper the fruit the better the jam, indeed the commercial grower, who likes to skin the cream off the market with his dessert raspberries, becomes quite affectionately disposed towards the jam-maker with his lower prices when, after a couple of wet days following a Sunday, he sees his raspberry rows bowed down with over-ripe fruit simply crying for the jam-tub.

Diseases of Raspberries,

Mosaic.   The variety Lloyd George, with its wonderful powers of raising cane, from which, ft is said, its name was derived, is probably giving place to Norfolk Giant, an inferior variety but an easier one to grow.   Some twenty years ago a friend of mine, who stood about 6 ft. 9 ins. high, planted many acres of the former variety.   In the early days of his planting I have seen him over-topped by the canes.   He extended his acreage to about 120 acres, necessitating thousands of pickers. Ten years later the canes had dropped to knee height and to-day they are no longer grown but some 70 acres of Norfolk Giant replace them.   I expect to see these replaced in a few years' time.

As can be seen from this instance, original vigour was not maintained, and established plantations gradually developed patches of cane bearing mottled leaf, the resultant stunting being common throughout the whole country (Plate X). From a strong grower it became, in many places, a very weak one.   Only when free from the mottled leaf or where prompt steps were taken to rogue the raspberry rows carefully in

summer and to dig up and burn the infected specimens could
robust stocks of Lloyd George be maintained or rebuilt. It
is on the practice of rigorous selection that the nurseryman
of to-day must rely, and there can be no doubt at all that
stocks from which canes are dug for sale and distribution
should be under strict Government supervision, even at the risk
of increasing our already redundant Civil Service.

Mosaic is a "virus" disease. It is easier to say what a virus
does than to describe the virus itself. It is as potent in an
evil way as the vitamin is beneficial. Both can be extracted
in a pure crystalline form. The varieties Superlative (now
seldom seen), and Lloyd George are very susceptible to infection. Baumforth B, though very slow to become affected, is
badly damaged once the infection becomes established.
Highly resistant is Pyne's Red Cross,[1] though it is usually
infected, and in spite of that remains sound and able to crop
well. Preussen is a carrier of virus but is highly virus-tolerant,
while Mitchell's Seedling[1] is very susceptible. There is no
cure for the disease. No soil disinfectant or spray can be
of any help but, where infected canes have been dug from an
otherwise sound row, it is essential to clear out the fibrous
root thoroughly from the gap and to replant with sound stock.

Though virus disease is rampant among British-grown
raspberries there are still countries where this trouble does not
occur. A friend visiting New Zealand in 1944 told me of
heavy crops of Red Antwerp and Lloyd George on canes over
7 ft. high. Plants of these varieties are now being tested in
England. In Kenya also raspberries seem free of trouble.

A virus disease can appear out of the blue when conditions
are suitable. Have we supplied such conditions by years of
artificial manuring? The scientist does not know, the compost
enthusiast says "Yes." I hesitate to express an opinion.

It is a very fortunate fact that the virus diseases are not
spread by seed. There have long been two schools of thought
on the subject of growing virus-free raspberries. One holds
that new seedlings should be obtained by suitable crosses and
worked up into stocks by "clonal" reproduction. This simply
means collecting the spawn thrown up by the original plant
and reproducing the same variety by planting up such spawn.
The other school holds that one can arrive at a suitable cross,
take unlimited seed and plant it out, thus raising a fruiting
cane just as rapidly as by planting a clonal cane, cutting

[1] Both are almost unobtainable to-day.

down after planting and letting the resulting shoots bear fruit. Canes raised from seed are not identical with the parents. Back ancestry comes out, and one Lloyd George cross, for example, will always throw a proportion of yellow-berried fruits. In spite of this Mr. Crane of the John Innes Institution who is testing these seedlings against the old types of clonal strains such as Lloyd George and Norfolk Giant says that one can raise virus-free seedlings which crop as heavily as the best, and though there are variations they are all red, so what does it matter? Better a little variety and a healthy strain than uniformity and likely early collapse.

Diseases.

There are several fungus diseases which can at times do much damage and are aided in their attack by weather, soil conditions, shade and insect attack.

Cane Blight is a fungus disease which affects some varieties more than others. It can be very bad on Lloyd George but even worse on Newburgh. When this promising raspberry was tried out at Wisley by the R.H.S. early in the war cane blight very nearly wiped out the variety. Present also on the canes was a big infestation of cane midge, a small fly which emerges from the soil in late April to lay eggs in the very young growing cane when this is no more than a few inches above the soil, and again later in the summer.

The development of the maggots of the midge splits the bark of the growing cane and opens it to infection by the cane blight fungus. It was reasoned therefore that if the midge could be controlled maybe the fungus would not gain admission. Two years' control of the midge by spraying with D.D.T. and Lime Sulphur has given complete control, and now Newburgh may again be regarded as a promising variety. I have seen the same result elsewhere and have had the same control in my own garden, using D.D.T. and Bouisol at the end of April, in mid-May and again immediately after fruit was picked.

Cane blight is to be found at the base of the cane at the end of the season. A diseased cane shows the base bark split and ragged with the thin covering of the bark peeling away. If examined carefully you will find dead sections of cane with clusters of little, round, black dots visible to the naked eye. These are the fruiting stage of the cane blight fungus and canes so affected will usually collapse and die instead of breaking into bud in the spring.

More common is Cane Spot, which begins in early June as small spreading purple spots on the young growing canes. As the spots increase in size the centres fade to white. Eventually these spots turn into cankers and next season throw out fungus spores which will re-infect. Where the attack is bad canes are weakened, fruit can be deformed, tips may be killed and a reduction in crop result.

Cane Spot can be controlled by spraying with Bouisol at makers' recommended strength or by Lime Sulphur applied at a strength of one quart of Lime Sulphur to five gallons of water when the fruit buds are breaking into growth in Spring and again just before blossoming again, using Bordeaux Mixture, Bouisol or Lime Sulphur at one pint to six gallons of water.

Other diseases of raspberries may affect the leaf and fruit, but the use of Lime-Sulphur or copper wash, as recommended above, will act as an insurance against most fungus troubles and is worth employing as a matter of routine. Such troubles are, however, largely seasonal.

Insect Pests.

The Raspberry Beetle. There are several important pests which attack the raspberry, but the most damaging, the most neglected, and the most simple to control, is the raspberry beetle. This pest will begin by damaging a few fruits early in the life of the raspberry patch but, if not noticed, it will, in a few years, build up to such an infestation that it will ruin the crop. (In 1942 the beetle was not unduly prevalent.) Twenty years ago, before the introduction of Derris as an insecticide, many an acre of fine strong canes was rooted up and burned because of the uncontrollable attacks of this beetle. To-day there is no excuse for anyone suffering from it, since in addition to Derris we have the even more powerful D.D.T., which if properly employed will give 100 per cent. immunity.

The raspberry beetle attacks in addition loganberries and allied plants and the cultivated blackberries. As a rule the housewife (unless she happens to be short-sighted) first makes its acquaintance when eating ripe raspberries and cream, as a little wriggling grub. Later it is seen as a scum of boiled specimens upon the top of the bottled fruit. In its adult stage the beetle is $\frac{1}{8}$ in. long and a pale, shiny brown. As soon as the raspberry flowers open you can look for it travelling around just inside the cup of the flower below the white stamens and pollen-bearing anthers (Plate XIX). Usually it will pre-

tend to be dead when you look for it and can be picked out of
or shaken off the flower. If, in a quarter of an hour, you can
find a few you may be sure that a spray or a dust with Derris
will be worth while to prevent those bleached drupes on the
side of the berry and the corpses in the bottled fruit.

Derris dust will not kill the bees, so for their sake it is
advisable to use Derris dust or D.D.T. for the flower application in early June followed by a good Derris wash mid to end
of June, when the flowers are over and the fruit is set.

This pest also attacks loganberries and allied varieties and
can be tackled at the same time but, in the case of the cultivated
blackberries, it should be sprayed for in the first, or the first
and third weeks of July (in the southern half of the country),
as the flowers are later.

Weevils.

Several weevils attack raspberries, eating flowers and fruit
and cutting holes in leaves and shoots. They are all very
hard to deal with and poison baits, using the American
formula of 5 lb. of raisins, $\frac{1}{2}$ lb. of fluosilicate and 5 lb. of
bran, would be quite impossible to-day, in our phoney Peace
period where puddings and poultry must take pride of place
over any weevil in creation. To-day D.D.T., which is easily
obtainable, will control most if not all of the damaging weevil
varieties. There is, however, one thing in common with the
three chief offenders, the red-legged, the clay-coloured and
the vine weevils—they all like good winter quarters. Rubbish
in hedgerow bottoms, in ditches and unburned piles of sticks,
old raspberry canes and so forth, are all favoured spots and
should be cleaned out or fired, thus depriving the pests of
their shelter. Canes, after fruiting, should be cut off at ground
level and not left as hollow dry stumps. It seems likely that
D.D.T. will attend to these pests.

The Raspberry Moth.

Sometimes the little red grubs of this moth, feeding on the
soft internal pith of shoots which they have entered by boring
a hole just below a bud, kill the shoot above their point of
entry and thus draw attention to their presence. Such dead
shoots if explored may yield the little red grub or the brown
chrysalis from which the moth will, in due time, emerge.

It is stated that in Scotland this is now the most serious pest attacking the raspberry. While met with in the English plantations it is not widespread or serious as a rule.

Where this pest does damage there is good reason to believe that it can be completely controlled by watering the soil around the canes with a Tar-Oil spray at 8´ per cent concentration, applied in December or January.[1]

Aphis.

I am told that this pest is of no consequence on raspberries, but having seen the rapid spread of mosaic disease on some acres of raspberries which were attacked by aphis I consider that any sucking insect is under suspicion as a carrier, and since the 8 per cent Tar-oil wash recommended for raspberry moth will entirely prevent the hatch of aphis eggs the certainty of controlling two pests with one wash is worth mentioning. Unfortunately, several varieties of aphis may attack the raspberry and all but one do so as summer migrants from wild blackberries and a variety of other hosts on which their eggs are laid. One cannot expect to control aphis by spraying in winter unless their eggs can be wetted with the spray, and if their eggs are away off in the hedgerows the winter-washer of raspberries may be wasting his time and his wash. It seems certain that control by summer spraying is difficult and uncertain in its results.

[1] This information emanates from Dutch research workers and is quoted in *Pests of Fruit and Hops* (Massee). I am now told that Tar-oil has little effect in our country. Keeping the canes clear of dead stubs from previous pruning and general hygiene should be helpful.

XII

STRAWBERRIES

Foreword.

THIS chapter has been heavily revised in December 1947 in order to bring it up to date. So far as the strawberry and the raspberry are concerned these fruits are now passing out of the dark days of virus infection and collapse into a brighter period of regenerated stocks and controlled propagation. Only by such painstaking methods as those employed by our research workers can the old vigour of the delectable strawberry be brought back and maintained. A great deal of work has been done and many lessons learned in the past ten years. In this revision I have drawn largely from Bulletin No. 95, Strawberries (H.M. Stationery Office, 2s. net), which was revised and re-issued in January, 1947.

Strawberries have always been a favourite fruit. Did not William Butler say in the seventeenth century: "Doubtless God could have made a better berry, but doubtless God never did" ? Their very botanical name Fragaria suggests a delicious aroma which the ripening berry most certainly has. Yet it is a curious fact that the scent of the ripe strawberry soon deteriorates into a stink if the fruit be shut up in a closed room. Scent and stench can be perilously near together, nor is this peculiar to the strawberry.

As we know them to-day the strawberry varieties are probably the result of crossing the two species emanating from Chile and Virginia respectively, though English and European types may also have been involved. Few of the old varieties remain, though we still have that popular sort Sir Joseph Paxton, introduced in 1862, and Royal Sovereign, which was introduced some thirty years later by Laxtons of Bedford. In 1872 you might have ordered from at least one reliable nurseryman no less than eighty-eight named varieties of strawberry.

Since those days many a fine variety has flourished and then faded away, for of late years this fruit has proved singularly susceptible to disease. It is therefore encouraging that Paxton and Sovereign still remain.

New Varieties.

During the post-war years considerable interest has been aroused by the seedlings known as the Cambridge varieties. Mr. D. Boyes, Director of the Horticultural Research Station at Cambridge, had, in the course of some seventeen years, produced thousands of new seedling varieties which had to be tried out in order to separate the winners from the duds. Some were quite obviously very promising. In 1944 he found himself short of space for testing purposes. Mr. Howard Jones, of Kingsley in Hants (I give his name to save myself from innumerable enquiries) a commercial grower of strawberry plants for the trade, took over some 680 of these new varieties and planted them out on trial. By June 1947 some forty-six varieties of outstanding promise had been selected and distributed for wider trial. These will no doubt be still further reduced in numbers, but first trials have proved some to be of excellent flavour, shape and colour, and able to crop very heavily indeed. A yield of seven tons an acre on two-year plants was obtained in one case, a comparative acreage of Royal Sovereign giving no more than three tons.

Last June (1947) I sampled a score or more of these new varieties which varied in flavour from fresh pineapple to pure turnip. Several needed three good bites to demolish and I admit I was impressed at their possibilities. Now research workers in strawberry problems do not approve of the early publication of results or the distribution of what to them are just untried strains of berry. In their opinion it will take ten to fifteen years to try out a new raspberry and at least four to five years to prove the value or otherwise of a new strawberry variety. Seedlings are free of virus diseases and so are usually very robust and prolific at first, but their immunity may be of short duration, and Science prefers to wait and see before expressing any definite opinion.

The strawberry is an odd fruit in that, unlike its companions in the garden, it carries its seeds outside. There seems no good reason why this should be so, and most other fruits tuck their seeds most carefully away. However, since the main idea of a luscious surround to a seed is to ensure that the fruit is eaten and the seed removed to a reasonable distance from the parent plant, the arrangement of the strawberry with regard to its seeds is a matter of small importance.

Sound seed development is just as important to the strawberry as any other fruit, for, without fertilised seed, the pulp will refuse to develop, and that is why some varieties of strawberry when planted alone as a result of imperfect fertilisation either fail to crop or produce berries with hard ends, green noses or thoroughly bad shape.

Strawberries grow and flourish all over the temperate world, but countries find their own particular varieties the best, and while American sorts look marvellous as pictured in the American fruit papers, I have yet to hear of any good Yankee variety which is worth growing commercially in England.

There is no doubt that our best English varieties take a deal of beating, though I have been assured that berries grown in Kashmir are even finer. However, this is no place for enlarging on the world's strawberries, interesting as the subject is. What does need enlarging on is our production of strawberries, for it seems to me that the supply becomes beautifully less with each succeeding year (in 1935 the commercial acreage stood at 26,752 acres: in early 1947 it is given as 10,500 with a tendency to rise), and the Strawberry Certification Scheme which the Ministry of Agriculture and the Research Stations have put into operation should ensure healthy plants for all, with some twenty-four varieties to choose from.

Sites for Strawberry Growing.

Strawberries, as everyone knows, grow and develop very near soil level. (An old fruit-picker once remarked to me: "Oh, sir, all I want to be happy is gooseberries without thorns, raspberries without leaves and strawberries without bending!"). Their lowly habit leaves them very much at the mercy of spring frosts, and since the biggest fruits develop from the early blossoms, the best crops over a period of years will always be from beds which are well up out of frosty lowlands. At the same time some surprising results can be secured in gardens by covering over a few rows with cloches or laying mats or straw loosely on top of the plants in late April and May when clear, calm nights suggest frost risk.

Frosting of the flower is indicated by a "black-eye," or centre, to the flower. This indicates death of the organs of fertility, and since the centre of the flower is occupied by the fruitlet, ready to develop after fertilisation has been satisfactorily effected, there can be no recovery from this damage. When frosts are only moderately severe (5° to 6° below freezing, on the ground) many opening blossoms and most unopened buds sheltered by leaf will escape, but, when one registers 8° to 10° of frost on the garden wall, as sometimes happens even in May, ground temperature is apt to be 5° to 7° lower still. So, in choosing a site for your strawberries, give preference to the highest part of your garden rather than the lowest and most sheltered part, such as a low corner backed by a bank which is in turn topped by a hedge.

Avoid, in any case, low places. Strawberries like a damp soil which, is also well drained, but they abominate water-logging and will not live under such conditions. Shade, in my opinion, provided it is only partial for part of the day, is preferred by them to full sun, for they are by nature woodland plants. Nearness to tall trees may also mitigate frost damage, but beware of soil robbery and droughting by such neighbours. A border behind a north wall is not to be despised, and very late fruits can be grown in such a situation despite almost complete lack of sun.[1]

Soil.

In this considerable latitude is permissible. Slight acidity is preferable to limey land; indeed there is no point in adding lime to a strawberry bed. Some sandy soils can be very useful and are to be preferred to soils on limestone or chalk which are apt to be shallow. On such soils chlorosis (which is equivalent to anæmia in the human being) causes loss of green pigment in the leaf and results in weak and unfruitful plants. The ideal is the medium to heavy, well-drained, deep loam.

It has been said that Royal Sovereign is best suited to the sandy loams, and in East Anglia I have seen punnets of choice berries of this variety picked by the ton from plants grown on sheer sand. These plants were never strawed; the grower used to put each basket under a tap to wash away any grit, relying upon the journey up to London to dry them off. It is a far cry from sand to clay, and in the days when strawberries

---

[1] A bed alongside a wall is useful for, on a radiation frost night, the wall prevents the loss of a great deal of heat from an area slightly wider than the wall and on both sides of it. When on frosty mornings I have to take train to London my mile to the station takes me downhill past a long garden wall bordering an asphalt path on the edge of a meadow. This meadow is a frost hole, and when hoar frost is present the meadow and the path are white with rime until one reaches the wall. Then a ten-foot wide stretch of path and grass is innocent of frost owing to the protection of the nine-foot wall.

were easier to grow, we used to look upon Sir Joseph Paxton as a heavy land berry and one of the very best, too, while Bedford Champion, another heavy land variety and once fairly popular, always struck me as a disgusting variety to eat, especially at about 4 a.m. on a summer morning, which is the crucial time for strawberry tasting. Slugs, however, which are invariably excellent judges, seemed to prefer it to Paxton, so maybe my taste was at fault.

On shallow, limestone soils such as one finds in the Cotswolds, strawberries seem to have a short life and to crop lightly, though I recall an acre of Paxtons which carried in its first fruiting year nearly 4 tons to the acre and then collapsed completely. On really heavy Herefordshire clay— that wonderful soil overlying the old red sandstone which has made the county famous for its fruit and farming—Stirling Castle used to be an amazing cropper. I recall a crop of this little strawberry on a Herefordshire fruit farm during World War I which yielded over 4 tons to the acre (a phenomenal yield for the variety which could not possibly be matched to-day).

The Need for Humus.

Grubbed woodland has always been chosen for strawberry planting where the choice was available, probably because the strawberry is known to need much humus in the soil. No soil, even though it has housed a muck-heap for a generation, can be too rich for a strawberry bed. Twenty years ago immense dressings of farmyard manure were a regular preliminary to strawberry planting. Fifty tons to the acre was by no means an exceptional dressing, and there is good reason to suppose that a ton of dung in those days was worth several tons of the modern litter from town stables. Even to-day, in the best of strawberry-growing districts, such dressings alone can be relied upon to produce heavy yields, and when one considers that the highest annual average yield per acre recorded for England and Wales was no more than 29·1 cwt. (in 1931), to raise a 4-ton-to-the-acre crop is no mean achievement, though the variety Huxley has been credited with six tons to the acre. The days of heavy and regular manuring were the days of heavy yields and of beds which lasted seven to ten years. One cannot help feeling that many of our present troubles may be due to diminished stamina, brought about by reduced feeding and unsuitable "ersatz" substitutes, resulting in strains which are unable to resist disease as did their fore-bears and which crop for a couple of seasons and then give up the ghost.

So, for the strawberry patch, the planter is advised to collect all the farmyard manure possible, all the local leaf mould in a ripe and mouldering state, and all the garden compost, and to double-dig his soil, incorporating a generous supply of these good things into his top 2 ft. but taking most particular care not to bring his bottom soil up to the top or vice versa. One must enrich the whole depth which is dug, but it must retain its original position.

Where one is doubtful as to the adequacy of the manurial preparation and is short of manure, additions of such bulky substances as shoddy or hop manure can be dug in, and Peruvian Guano, hoof and horn, steamed bone, bone meal and meat and fish meals can all be worked in during the growing season with a hoe. In trials in Kent meat and bone meal has proved superior to artificials and dried blood and hoof and horn. One very successful Kent grower considers that all the manure for a strawberry bed should go in before planting and that later additions are valueless.

Varieties of Strawberry.

In 1935 the strawberries selected and recommended by Mr.

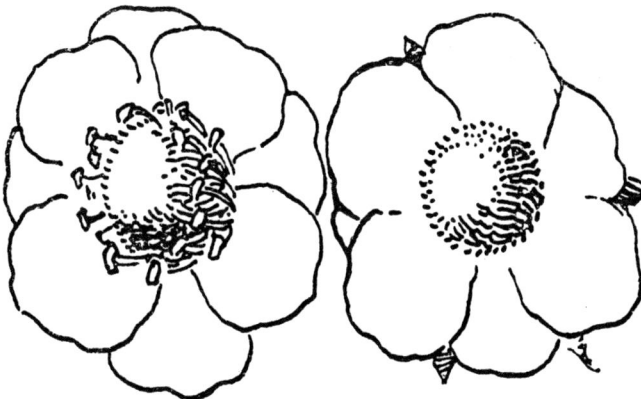

THE SELF-FERTILE BLOOM OF ROYAL SOVEREIGN.

THE SELF-STERILE BLOOM OF TARDIVE DE LEOPOLD.

A. N. Rawes, who was then in charge of the fruit side of the Royal Horticultural Society's Gardens at Wisley in Surrey, as suitable for amateur culture were four in number: Royal Sovereign, Sir Joseph Paxton, Oberschlesien and Tardive de Leopold. He did not recommend those excellent varieties, British Queen, Dr. Hogg, Givons' Late Prolific and Noble, because as he said "It is so difficult to obtain healthy, vigorous and pure stock." At that, as Mr. Quentin Reynolds would say, "He spilled a mouthful".

That was twelve years ago, and I doubt if Mr. Rawes would contradict me if I said that of the four, Oberschlesien, as a notorious carrier of virus disease, is to-day not really good enough to associate with the first named two, in which case we are left with but three for our garden. But Tardive is self-sterile, which means that if you plant it all alone, as many a hundred gardeners have, you will see it flower but fruits will be few and far between and poor in size and shape. With Sovereign as a neighbour it will fruit admirably. Both Sovereign and Paxton are self-sterile and can be grown alone or together, but it is not always wise to grow two varieties unless one is sure of one's stock.

Mr. Charles H. Oldham, referring to strawberries at the end of 1944, recalled that in 1920 the Royal Horticultural Society arranged at Wisley a trial of forty-eight strawberry varieties. To-day only six of those varieties exist.

Now let us bring this more up to date. Dr. W. S. Rogers of East Malling Research Station in Kent, who has probably devoted more time to research on this fruit than anyone else, gave it as his opinion in 1940 that the best thing for the amateur to do would be to plant one bed of Royal Sovereign by itself. If a succession was needed then a second bed could be planted as far away as possible from the first with Tardive de Leopold pollinated by Huxley. There is no doubt that where strawberries are difficult to grow Huxley is the safest choice, and it can be planted by itself.

The Importance of Strain.

Between the two World Wars a good deal of work was done in regard to variety and strain of strawberries. I do not propose to weary you with figures, but four strains of Royal Sovereign collected and planted in Hampshire gave the following yields per acre:

Strain	1924		1925		1926	
	cwt.	lb.	cwt.	lb.	cwt.	lb.
A. ..	6	58	41	68	51	28
C. ..	4	12	30	60	18	64
D. ..	7	36	23	44	35	100
E. ..	6	28	19	42	5	60

(Taken from Ministry of Agriculture Bulletin, *Strawberries*, 1937, by C. H. Oldham.)

These are interesting figures, for they show how strain A went from strength to strength and was probably perfectly good for a fourth crop, while strain C was fit for little after its second year and strain E collapsed completely with a smaller crop in its third year than its first.

In Devonshire, Sovereign strains behaved just as erratically and from plants set out in 1928 and crop recorded in 1930 individual strains yielded as high as 29 cwt. 11 lb. to the acre and as low as 7 cwt. 41 lb.

Ensuring a Sound Strain.

Having realised the vital importance of strain you will very rightly ask: "How may I ensure this?" and regretfully I must reply: "It can't be done". I realize that this is not helpful. All that Science can do in the way of warm-water treatment of runners, thus clearing out the infecting aphis and tarsonemus mite, is merely palliative. Every intrusive greenfly is a potential carrier of the infernal virus diseases. By purchasing "certified" plants one can make a good start, but I have seen the best-looking plants go down to 'crinkle' and 'yellow edge disease' and collapse before ever a fruit was picked (Plates XI and XII). I was told that there happened to be "gypsies in the wood" in the shape of wild strawberry plants in a nearby coppice and that the infection came from them, but recent research suggests that the virus-carrying strawberry greenfly does not attack the wild strawberry. Against that I can tell of superb plants, vigorous and prolific after seven years of cropping. At times one comes across happy, healthy plants of a forgotten variety overgrown with weeds and rubbish in some deserted garden. All that one can do is to get the best plants available, manure your ground really well, cultivate and spray and thoroughly deserve success—whether you will achieve it seems to be largely a matter of luck. Personally, I never expect a better lot of berries than the first year of fruiting or a heavier weigh than the second season's yield. After that one should have another patch of one-year-olds ready to carry on the good work.   Most people plant a patch, crop it till a few miserable plants remain and then grumble because they have to buy strawberries.

Planting.

Investigation seems to show that summer planting in July–August gives the finest plants and best results. September planting is better than planting in October. From then on no planting must be done, and it is a fact that it is better to plant in March–April than in October. You have, therefore, the periods July–September and March–April for strawberry planting.

The ground having been well and truly double-dug and manured should be well firmed by planting time.   Soil should be friable and in nice working condition.   For the four varieties mentioned rows should be 2 ft. 6 ins. apart and plants should be 18 ins. apart in the rows.   In good soil Huxley can be allowed 3 ft. between the rows and 2 ft. 6 ins. between the plants in the row.   This allows ample room.   It is a great mistake to crowd plants and rows together, for this induces weaker plants, smaller crops and quicker collapse.

Plants should be examined, and if roots are long they can be trimmed to a reasonable length, which makes for easier planting.   Where extra fine plants from pots are planted trimming of roots is unnecessary, the whole root content of the pot being planted with a minimum of disturbance.   A trowel is the best tool to plant with; the roots should be spread out in the hole, taking care to plant on a little mound at the base of the hole so that the central cluster or crown of the runner remains above ground.   One can afford these niceties in the case of a few plants.   As each row is planted tread the soil really firmly around the plants and then run a hoe or prolonged cultivator along the rows and between the plants, but no nearer to a plant than 2 ins. or the soil will be loosened and the firming effect lost.   This firmness in planting is essential to rooting since roots must grow against pressure.   Successful growers have told me that for growing strawberries they like a soil which sets like concrete, provided they can cultivate down the rows and retain the moisture.

The First Winter.

Frosts lift the top soil and plants which have no deep roothold lift with it. When the frost goes plants may be left loose upon the top; therefore, when winter frosts are over and the ground is reasonably dry, repeat the treading and the hoeing.

The First Spring and Summer.

From March on the hoe is the best weapon to use. If weather is dry a mulch of short, rotten manure will help to save moisture and rains will wash down its fertility. If weather later on is dry and watering is done do not turn a hose on the patch but draw out a hollow between each plant in the row, fill each hollow with water and let it soak in. Then draw up dry soil to cover the damp spot and prevent cracking and loss of soil moisture.

If your planting was in July–August and your plants were from pots you can crop them in moderation the first year. Where this is done limit the blossom trusses to one per plant and keep all runners pinched off. Straw will be needed round each plant to keep the berries up and out of reach of splashed mud or grit in wet weather.

Where autumn and spring plantings were made there should be no attempt to secure fruit the first year. Plant strength must be conserved to build up a strong crown for the serious business of the second year when fine fruit should be forthcoming. Hoeing should be continued in suitable weather and, as far as is possible, every weed should be kept away. Some weeds are 'host' plants for pests. Light applications of organic fertilisers can go on during the growing season, using a mere sprinkle before hoeing. Runners should be kept cut off unless a row of plants is used for raising fresh stock. In autumn a dressing of farmyard manure or compost can be spread over the whole bed and can be lightly turned in, but only down the centres between the rows. The plants themselves should not be dug round or interfered with.

Second Year Treatment.

In the second year, from plump crowns, a fine show of blossom trusses should be forthcoming. Protection against frost should be considered if you are in a low-lying area. If you have enough cloches to cover a row be prepared to do so. If you have any old hessian strips, black-out curtains or light mats, keep them handy to cover a few square yards when the night is calm and cool and the stars are bright.

Old growers used to say that early strawing drew frost damage and did not protect the plants. In many cases they were right. If cold air at freezing temperature is draining on to and over a strawberry field with a nice slope which is not strawed it will pass away like water at an inch or so depth between the rows of plants, provided that these are clear of weeds and run with the fall of the land. If, however, the rows are loosely strawed, the air-drainage flow will only begin when the cold air has accumulated to a depth greater than the height of straw and the plants, and so all night they will lie submerged in a shallow layer of cold air. But we are not dealing with a field of strawberries, and circumstances alter cases. If you heap straw over your garden plants and not under them you will gain some measure of protection against direct radiation loss and you can pull it off again easily enough when the sun is warm in the morning.

Speeding Ripening.

Straw delays ripening, since it is light in colour and so reflects the sunlight in place of absorbing it. If you could dye your straw black you could speed up ripening considerably. I have tried a wide strip of brown paper interleaved with bitumen, on the American "paper-mulch" lines, in place of straw and gained a week in ripening, but paper of this sort is still unobtainable. A row of cloches, applied in February, will give about three weeks' earlier ripening in Southern counties, since glass admits the heat rays yet prevents re-radiation loss to a great extent.

One should be careful with straw, for much noxious weed may be spread by it and thistles, in particular, are hard to get rid of. Wheat and oat straw is preferable to barley, which latter though easier to tuck in contains as a rule far more grain than wheat straw and in my experience is often infested with vermin and thistle seeds ; careful hoeing and collection of weeds should precede the strawing. The system is to walk down the rows dropping the straw and then to pull and tuck it in under the trusses of swelling fruit, taking particular care not to break them. Strawing should be finished while the berries are green and not left till they begin to ripen. When you pick your fruit do so in the morning while it still holds the coolness of the night and, if you wish your choice specimens to keep for a day or two, pick always by the stalk and do not handle the fruit itself.

Birds.

Our "feathered songsters" can be a perfect curse. Blackbirds, thrushes and starlings all consider that strawberries belong to them and if allowed will become tame enough to share them with you. A cage is a very extravagant method of saving the crop from their depredations, for it can only serve for some four weeks. Fish netting, which, after a few weeks can be bundled up and stowed away till next year, is a far cheaper proposition.

One lives and learns. I have tried posts and wires and somehow the netting always got hung up. A doctor sent me a new idea. He drives 3 ft. stakes into the soil parallel with the rows, so that a taut string tied six inches below the top of each post lies along and above the row of plants. The stakes can project 18 ins. out of the soil. He then places a jam pot upside down on each stake and the net will draw over them perfectly. As a result there were no obstructions to catch the net meshes and it slid easily along the wires when pushed back for picking. When ordering fish-netting one should remember that the measurements given in the advertisements are of ultimate possible stretch and that to cover a given area at least double the advertised width should be ordered. Few things are more annoying than to find you have underestimated your air protection and have left your flank open to attack by the enemy.

Post-Crop Treatment.

When the strawberries are over and you have heaved your last sigh of regret there is little to do save to roll up the netting on a dry day, and to cut off all the old leaves and runners and weeds and then rake them off with the straw to put them on the compost heap. Or, if you prefer, you may burn the lot and return the ashes to the soil. This can be done on the bed if the leaf and straw are dry and there is a brisk breeze to spread the burning. The bed can then be hoed and cleaned up prior to the spreading of a mulch of manure, or compost, in the autumn, and light digging down the rows. On no account allow the whole patch to be dug, as this weakens and damages the plants. Under the head of fungus diseases you will find some suggestions for dusting and spraying which I will not repeat.

Strawberry Plant Propagation.

Although the commercial propagation of certifiable plants

demands isolation and not cropping the plants from which runners are taken the amateur can be a little less fussy. Select only the strongest plants with sound flower trusses in their first year as parents for your new stock. At all times runners which do not show a flower truss in their first year should be hoed out and destroyed. Having assured yourself that your parent plant has a flower truss, pinch it out. (This sounds rather like a recipe which begins: "Take a dozen eggs, break them and throw them away"). Keep the row of parent runners well hoed and never allow them to be short of water. Give them the same attention as the main bed with regard to sulphur dusting and spraying with nicotine. In early July runners will be forming and ready to root. Take a number of 3-in. pots—commercially known as 60's—cover the hole in the bottom with a nice flat crock to deny entry to the worms and allow for drainage, and fill each tightly to within $\frac{1}{2}$ in. of the top with a rich mixture consisting of one part good fibrous loam to one part of old rotted cow manure (failing that compost, leaf mould, etc.). Add a good sprinkle of sharp sand and a few handfuls of bone meal to a barrow load. Now bury the pots so that soil level inside the pot coincides with that outside and peg down the first runners into the pots, using a bit of stick or laying a stone atop of it. Allow each plant no more than five runners or you may reduce next season's fruit crop and, once the runner has begun to root, cut the exploring end off some 3 ins. beyond the pot, leaving the attachment to the parent plant untouched. These new plants should be watered and looked after. An occasional dose of Peruvian Guano followed by water will keep them growing strongly. Normally, from a month to five weeks will see the pots full of roots and the young plant can then be severed from the parent to begin life on its own.

A better and easier system than pots, for runners raised for one's own use, is to lay a double line of bricks with a 4-in.

Potted runner. A. Self-rooted. C. Note stalks at B. where bloom buds were removed.

space between the rows of bricks between the rows of plants you wish to propagate. Fill the space in with a mixture of one part loam, three of old cow manure and half-part silver or good sharp sand and make firm. Runners can then be pegged down on to this. Being well above soil level they get full light and the bricks prevent weed competition. Watering is easy and when plants are wanted in August and September the bricks are removed and the plants can be cut out in squares of root and compost.

If a new bed is to be made, then stout, well-rooted plants will be available from these pots to be set out in July or August in the best possible condition to fruit the summer following. If disbudded in April-May after planting, exceptionally strong plants for fruiting in their second year will be formed.

Such plants are, of course, ideal for forcing in the greenhouse, but this practice in war-time is not one to be encouraged. We have seen that three weeks can be gained by using cloches and while these have always seemed to me excessively high in price I am told by the makers that this is not so, that in war-time the right wire is very difficult to obtain, glass is expensive and labour also. Readers will, therefore, please themselves whether they buy complete cloches or buy the components and make a possibly less workmanlike job with their own hands. A very sound idea if you have plenty of empty glass jam jars is to put the individual flower trusses as soon as flowers have set to fruits into the jam jars, laying them down horizontally. These are in effect cloches, but take care that the swelling fruit does not prevent withdrawal of the truss from the bottle, for splintered glass is no substitute for sugar.

Back Yard Strawberry Growing.

It is, of course, possible to grow plants in 6-in. or 8-in. pots on window-sills or in window-boxes, but the time occupied by the plants for their brief period of fruiting does not suit most people. For those who have no room for a strawberry bed the barrel method of cultivation, occupying as it does no more than a square yard, may have its appeal.

For barrel planting strong August-taken runners must be used so that fruit will be had the first season after planting. In an average 40-gallon barrel, which is about 76 ins. around its equator, three rows of holes 2½ ins. in diameter are bored

24 Strawberries to a sq. yard.

with an auger, six holes to the row. The top row and the
bottom row will lie between the second and third hoops which
hold the barrel together, and the third row will be around
the centre. The centre row of holes should be arranged so
that these fall between the upper and lower rows of holes
and not in vertical line with them. Six 1-in. holes should also
be bored in the bottom of the barrel for drainage.

Having mixed up the soil, using the same mixture as
recommended for rooting runners, the barrel should be raised
from the ground by standing it on six bricks spaced around
its base. Before putting the soil into the barrel cover the
bottom with 2 ins. of broken brick or tile. Now begin filling
in, but while doing so, stand a section of 6-in. drain pipe (or
a piece of stout cardboard bent into a pipe will do) in the
centre of the barrel, filling this pipe with broken brick and

bringing up the level of soil around it. As you reach the level of the first row of holes see that your soil is well firmed and insert the plants as shaken from the pot, from the inside, pushing the leaf and crown gently through the opening until the mass of root butts up against the barrel side. Plant very firmly and water each layer of plants before continuing to raise the soil level. By lifting the central section of drainpipe, or cardboard tube, a core of porous brick will be left behind which will allow effective aeration of the soil. When the top of the tub is reached another six plants can be set out there, thus providing twenty-four plants on a single square yard of occupied space.

This system of strawberry growing, if the tub is in a sheltered place with a sunny aspect, will provide ripe fruit about a week earlier than the outdoor bed. Much of the success will depend upon soil consistency, and your ability to prevent the soil from drying out. Watering is done from the top and the soil, though rich, must be porous yet retentive. A balance is achieved by the ratio of well-rotted manure to sand in the potting soil.

Be careful when buying your barrel that it has not contained creosote. A tar barrel is all right, for this can be burned out by setting fire to the loose tar with a newspaper torch and rolling the barrel when it is well alight. For real permanence the oak wine cask is best of all.

The Terrace Method.

It was, I believe, the wily Japs who invented the terrace method of growing. This is arrived at by facing a steep five foot slope of rich soil with square stone tiles with one corner knocked off. Plants are set in the interstices between the tiles. Such plants will be well ventilated and should keep free of mould, mildews and slugs, all serious foes of the strawberry. These terraces can also be covered over with mats at night, thereby speeding up growth and ensuring earlier crops. A series of such terraces would give a handsome yield and fruit quality should be high, bird protection easy, and the idea may appeal to some enthusiastic backyarder who is tired of experimenting with hydroponic soil-less culture.

Strawberries are quite easy to produce in a cold greenhouse. All one needs are good plants in pots and shelves near the glass. Plants must be kept free of pests such as aphis and spider. Nicotine spraying will attend to the former

\nd a little sulphur dust beneath the leaf will keep down the latter.

Perpetual Fruiting Strawberries.

These carry moderate sized fruits in the summer, and if the main parent plant is allowed to form a few runners and is limited to the first produced, each runner will provide fruit in late autumn which will ripen till frosts cut it down. These fruiting runners can be taken up in spring and set out to provide parent plants for the following summer while the original plant is dug up and thrown away. A regular sequence is thus arranged for.

Alpine Strawberries.

These pretty little fruits are either very much liked or considered hardly worth picking. Certainly the addition of white wine relieves them of any tendency to dryness, but white wine has an appeal of its own. They are very easy to grow since they are readily raised from seed, though some few varieties can be raised from their runners; others make compact plants and bear no runners (Plate XIII). Some varieties will make quite big plants—larger than the Royal Sovereign in the case of Baron Solemacher—but the true French Alpines are compact, moderate growers. Manure, while appreciated, is less essential than liberal supplies of water in dry spells, since the plants fruit from July to late autumn. Although liable to become carriers of virus trouble the plants will continue to bear for several years under good treatment. For this reason it is inadvisable to mix Alpines with other strains, and since birds trouble them but little, they can be planted as a border to a flower bed. Seed can be sown in spring or autumn and the little plants pricked out to grow on to be planted in permanent quarters in summer or spring.

Varieties of Strawberry.

Bulletin No. 95, Strawberries, was revised in 1947 by a galaxy of research stars, and they brought down the number of *universally* recommended varieties to three. These are Royal Sovereign, Madame Lefebvre and Huxley. Of these Royal Sovereign is outstandingly the best.

This offers no great choice and it is of interest to glance at a typical trade list of available strawberry varieties. It is possible to obtain from the trade or the retail nurseryman, Royal Sovereign, Early Cambridge, Western Queen, The Duke, Fillbasket, Huxley Giant, Little Scarlet, Perle de Prague, Scarlet

Queen, Sir Joseph Paxton, Tardive de Leopold, Oberschlesicn, an Alpine variety or two, and St. Fiacre, an autumn fruiter. Among those which have fallen by the wayside we must include Bedford Champion, British Queen, Givons' Late Prolific, Dr. Hogg and Noble.

The varieties mentioned above may be described as under.

Royal Sovereign. (Preferably Malling 40 strain). Raised and introduced by Laxton's of Bedford in 1892. Early. A reasonably strong grower according to strain. Self fertile. By far the best all round variety. Very large fruits from the early blooms if protected from frost to which the variety is very sensitive owing to its habit of growth. Susceptible to Virus disease. D.J.C.

Early Cambridge. A variety raised by Sir R. Biffin at Cambridge and introduced in 1937. Early. Growth vigorous. Tolerant to Virus disease. Self fertile and a late bloomer. This and its habit of growth which covers the flowers protects it from frost. The fruit is medium to large and the colour a good red. D.J.

The Duke. Raised and introduced by Laxton's of Bedford in 1919. Early. A moderately vigorous upright plant. The fruit is medium to small in size and pale red in colour. Hardly worth growing to-day.

Fillbasket. Another variety raised by Laxton's of Bedford and resulting from a cross between Royal Sovereign and Latest of All was introduced by them in 1898. A fertile variety and still growing good plants. Fruit medium in size pale but sweet.

Huxley (M. 44). This variety masquerades under many aliases, Evesham Wonder, Evesham Giant or No Name, Brenda Gautrey, etc. It came from California into England about 1912. Main crop. A very vigorous grower with glossy green leaves which give good protection to its flowers against frost. Apt to come a bad shape and poor colour in wet seasons and leaf may have to be cut away to aid in ripening. Flavour and consistency both poor as compared with Royal Sovereign, but it makes good jam. It is very tolerant to virus disease. J.

Madam Kooi. Introduced from Holland in the twenties, this berry was once largely grown and is still advertised in the daily press. Main crop. Fruit is enormous, rather light in colour and of banana-like consistency. More than two bites are needed to dispose of the average fruit. Plants are large and

E

leaves are able to afford some protection against frost. It is fairly tolerant of virus. **J.**

Madame Lefebvre. Introduced in 1923. Can be quite vigorous and likes a light or even chalky soil. Is grown well in East Sussex where it is a popular variety. Early. Tolerant to virus. Self fertile and of fair flavour. On wet soil suffers badly from Red Core disease.

Oberschlesien (M. 42). When introduced in 1924 was a fairly vigorous upright plant carrying a medium-sized shiny red berry. Although classed among the tolerant types virus played the very devil with this variety in the early thirties. It is now being regenerated. Main crop. Flowers are not fully fertile and a pollinator is needed. **D.J.C.**

Perle de Prague. Introduced from Czechoslovakia in 1939 by a Romsey grower Mr. C. Jessel. Early. The plant is vigorous and crops heavily. It is classed as an intermediate for virus. Flowers early and owing to its flat habit of growth in its first season is liable to frost damage. Fruit is medium to small, bright red with pink flesh. **D.C.**

Sir Joseph Paxton. Introduced in 1862. A vigorous grower with fair protection against frost. Main crop to late. Flowers self fertile and fruit large and a rich dark red when fully ripe. Flavour very good. Susceptible to virus infection. **D.J.C.**

Tardive de Leopold. Introduced in 1924. Strong grower with erect flower trusses which are quite infertile and must be cross pollinated by another variety. Late. Very sensitive to frost, but carries late opening buds which can be set with a growth hormone spray on the same lines as the tomato. Flavour passable when really ripe. **D.C.**

Western Queen. Introduced in 1934. Vigorous plant and an upright grower. Main crop. Self fertile. Fruit large and of fair quality. Is intermediate as regards virus. **D.C.**

Note. M. 40 after Royal Sovereign, M. 44 after Huxley, and M. 42 after Oberschlesien indicates that certificated plants in these varieties are from tested and inspected pedigree stocks.

D—Dessert.
J—Jam.
C—Canning.

Perpetual Fruiting Strawberries.

St. Antoine de Padoue, St. Fiacre and St. Joseph are three useful varieties and pleasant to eat. Fruit is medium to fair

size. Colour is good. Fruit can be had from summer to late
autumn and plants are not particular as to soil.

Alpine Strains.

Belle de Meaux, La Brillante, Gaillon Rouge, Baron
Solemacher (Plate XIII) are all good varieties. Large seedsmen usually offer seed of Alpine strawberries. Some do not
make runners. The wild wood strawberry transplanted into
good garden soil can be as good as most Alpines.

Strawberry Troubles

We have already discussed the importance of sound stock
or strain in strawberries, and this is indissolubly associated
with disease resistance. The two worst virus troubles—Yellow
Edge disease and Crinkle—are transmitted from infected to
healthy plants by greenflies, which having absorbed the virus
with the sap, become carriers of the disease as they feed on
plants which are free of it.

The Strawberry Aphis.

Even where no virus trouble is present the strawberry aphis
causes damage to the plant by its furious appetite for sap.
If you find that greenfly is present on the opening leaf, on
the under side of leaves and along the leaf stalks, some control
can be had by spraying thoroughly with a solution of ¼ oz.
pure nicotine, ¼ lb. of soft soap in 3 gallons of water. It
is sound practice when planting out runners which have been
bought from outside to dip each runner in this same insecticide,
thus making sure of a start clean from this particular pest.

With regard to the mite which attacks strawberries, this is
microscopic in size although the damage which it does is
considerable. Its activity cripples the plant which loses its
vigour and becomes stunted and unhappy. Control is very
difficult and never completely effective. The nicotine-soap
spray leaves it unmoved, but all mites object to sulphur, and
where the pest is bad the best prescription which one can offer
is a 3 per cent Lime-Sulphur wash in middle to late March.
(A 3 per cent wash means 1 qt. of Lime-Sulphur to 8 gallons of
water.)

Virus Diseases.

In most gardens a visit to the strawberry bed will show a
number of plants which are small and stunted and carry no

worthwhile fruit. An occasional survivor of the originally
vigorous plants may suggest to the gardener that a little liquid
or other manure may be needed to bring back the old product-
ivity, but the hope is a vain one. A virus-infected plant with
the disease fully developed can never be reinvigorated and the
only remedy is a fresh planting.

In June, 1947, Dr. Prentice of East Malling Research Station
was quite distressed at his inability to secure specimens of the
particular greenfly—*Capitophorus fragariae*—for experimental
purposes. The sub-zero temperatures of February of that year
had killed them off, though no doubt survivors will have started
a brave new world in good time for 1948.

It is of great importance to the strawberry grower to learn
that the "Yellow Edge" collapse of plants is not due to a single
virus but to a combination of two working together. It appears that the strawberry greenfly is the sole carrier of these two
viruses. The trouble may start with the virus known as "Mild
Crinkle", a slight crinkling of the young leaf which is visible
in early summer and may have little effect on cropping. There
is also a virus described as "Severe Crinkle" which is a very
much worse type of crinkle than the mild form. A greenfly
feeding on a plant affected with Mild Crinkle will absorb the
infection into its system and if it travels on to any clean strawberry plant within twenty-four hours it can pass on that
infection. The infection only persists for twenty-four hours.
But if the aphis sucks up the sap from a plant infected with
"Yellow Edge" virus it becomes infected for life. Suppose
now that an aphis infected with the virus of mild or severe
crinkle also collects an infection of Yellow Edge virus and moves
on to a clean plant and attacks that. The effect is dynamite
and the plant goes down to severe Yellow Edge virus and rapidly
becomes useless.

Symptoms of mild or severe Crinkle can be seen in the early
summer and Yellow Edge becomes obvious about September.

Control of Virus.

Obviously the first step is to plant virus-free plants if they
can be obtained and to control greenfly as far as possible by
dipping the plants before planting in a nicotine solution, by
spraying with nicotine before flowering and by maintaining
enough water in the soil at all times since drought conditions
always encourage greenfly. Virus-infected plants should be
removed and destroyed as soon as seen.

Weevils and Caterpillars.

When single leaves or trusses of flower on a strawberry plant wilt and collapse the cause is probably weevil damage to the stalk. The weevil concerned may be the greeny blue Rhynchites or the variety known as the Elephant Beetle or Needle Bug. The remedy for these two pests is to dust the plants with a 5 per cent D.D.T. dust during the first week in May, or a few days earlier if the season is a very forward one. This dust will also control any caterpillars which may be present.

Cockchafer Grubs.

The underground larvae of the Cockchafer, or May Bug, the large brown beetle which flies around hawthorn bushes in early summer, will often cause havoc when strawberries are planted after turf has been dug in. A friend of mine lost as many as 10 per cent of his plants the first season. The early symptoms of attack may vary from the wilting of a single leaf to the collapse of the whole plant. If immediate action be taken at the first sign of a flagging leaf and the plant is lifted out with a spade it is usual to find the big dirty white, brown-headed grub up to two inches long still busy at the roots. If the first signs are not noticed and the whole plant wilts it is usual to find that the grub has moved on and begun to attack a neighbouring plant, so that for this pest early detection is essential.

Occasionally a Ghost Swift moth caterpillar or a colony of them will attack from below ground and at times I have found a single wireworm esconced in the centre of the crown of an unhappy looking strawberry plant. These cannot be controlled.

Moulds and Mildews.

Mould or Botrytis is common in wet seasons, in shady places and on berries which are not strawed enough to keep the fruits from touching the soil. Fruits must be kept up off the ground, for if they rest upon it they will be bitten by various small slugs and insects. Spores of botrytis rot are floating in the air all summer waiting to attack any fruit with a perforated skin. Sulphur dusting will help to reduce mould infections, but far more important are exposure to sun and moving air.

Mildew on the other hand is a highly infective disease which begins as an underleaf infection in May. At first the leaves show dark spots on the top of the leaf. Later the leaf edges tend to curl upwards. The mildew spreads to stalks and fruit trusses and eventually on to the blossoms. Fruit also is attacked and fails to grow and drops off. The remedy is sulphur, either as a lime sulphur spray in mid April followed by sulphur dust or by using sulphur dust alone. Sulphur dust is harmless and can be applied at any time but must not be used during the fruit ripening period if the berries are to be bottled or canned.

Red Core Disease.

This trouble has come to the fore of late years and is of rather local incidence, being particularly prevalent where soil drainage is bad. The name describes the symptoms well enough, and if the dead or dying plant is lifted and the main root cut down vertically the red core or centre is easily seen. There are some new Scotch varieties called the Auchintruive Seedlings which are resistant to the disease. There is no remedy unless it be to drain the land.

Strawberry Leaf Spot.

There are two types of this. The reddish-brown spot which surrounds a grey centre is common and can often be found on the old leaf of runners sent out for planting. From these, infected leaves should be cut off and destroyed before planting. Infection is general and usual in wet districts and damp, stagnant atmospheres. While not serious, Leaf Spot debilitates, since it reduces effective leaf area and also attacks the stems of leaves. Sulphur dusting will help to reduce infection in spring and again when the old leaf has been cut away and the bed is tidied up for the autumn and winter.

Note.

Growers who are really keen on producing good strawberries should follow a preventive spraying and dusting programme. Beginning with dipping new plants in nicotine and soap solution at planting time, dusting the rows with sulphur can follow in Autumn and in April and May. During April the nicotine spray can be repeated, choosing a really warm day (nicotine does not vaporise effectively at low temperature) any time in the early part of the month. If Tarsonemus mite is known to be about, or even if it is not present, the suggested Lime-Sulphur spray in the middle of March can be applied as a general preventive. Lime-Sulphur cannot be used with soap as it curdles the mixture. Sulphur dust can be used at any time except during the picking season. If a mixture of Lime-Sulphur and nicotine is desired a "wetting agent" should be used to replace soap. The horticultural counter of the modern chemist's shop is well acquainted with this.

XIII

THE TOMATO

THIS fruit is now so popular and so firmly established as an outdoor plant that even those with no garden should try to grow it in pots on a sunny balcony or flanking the front doorstep.

Site.

While the ideal site is against a sheltered, sunny wall or solid wood fence, with an aspect between South and West, tomatoes will grow perfectly well and happily in the open provided that they are well supported. North and East walls are not suitable sites and if grown there much of the fruit will fail to ripen.

One recent catalogue intrigued me by detailing a method of producing earlier tomatoes by allowing the plants to lie flat on a mattress of straw set beneath a row of cloches. This may provide an "early bite" but it must take up a good deal of room, and cloches of a suitable size are expensive things, whereas a stick is cheap enough and the air is free.

Tomatoes love the sun. It is our lack of ultra-violet rays that rules out the hydroponic or soilless method of gardening from economic possibilities, though in California it may have its points. Where soil is poor, and the garden is apt to lose the sun early in the day, it is possible to set the plants in big pots and move these around to make the most of the sunshine. For filling pots good soil, suitably mixed with the essential ingredients, can usually be had from the local nurseryman at a reasonable charge.

Varieties to Grow.

Since the war cut down our tomato supplies a great deal of interest has been focussed on large scale trials carried out by such august bodies as the Royal Horticultural Society and repeated by various centres throughout the country. In 1941, with Mr. Middleton, I saw a really remarkable large-scale trial of varieties accommodated on what a year before had been parkland in the suburbs of Nottingham.

These trials are important, for, although the outdoor tomato has been grown in the Badsey and Evesham districts of Worcestershire for generations, it is of rather a specialised type and less like the greenhouse variety than are the modern outside types. The low price of tomatoes before the war also contributed to the neglect of tomato growing by the amateur with no greenhouse. This is a pity, for it has been stated that an outdoor-grown tomato contains twice the Vitamin C content of the indoor-grown fruit. This, of course, was easily remedied in peace time by eating two tomatoes instead of one, but now one tomato has to do the work of several, so the outdoor variety must at all cost be encouraged. Only by properly planned and tabulated trials can the best performers be selected from scores of competitors and be recommended for general planting. Even so, results will vary and five years or so will be needed for completely reliable statistics to be collected and conclusions reached. Every seedsman offers a large choice of varieties, his own, quite naturally, being the best. An independent official trial saves much argument, especially when it has been confirmed by repetition.

A Recent Trial.

The Royal Horticultural Society's Journal for March, 1942 contains a fairly full account of the yields of tomato varieties in an outdoor trial. It was carried out by the John Innes Horticultural Institution. Out of eighteen varieties grown (admittedly under ideal conditions) the first six are as follows, the figures in brackets being the average weight in pounds of fruit per individual plant: Harbinger (7·08), Stonor's Exhibition (7 00), Ailsa Craig (6·71), Stonor's Progress (6·58), Market King (6·54), Radio (6·37). The yield of these top six is high, for 8 lb. from a single plant is as much as one can expect from any outdoor-grown plant and 4 lb. to 5 lb. is a good crop. Weight, however, is not everything and for uniformity of shape, with fruits averaging six or eight to the pound, the following were reliable performers: Ailsa Craig, Stonor's Exhibition, Radio, Moneymaker (6·32), Sunrise (6·28), E.S.1 (5·88), and Plumpton King (4·92).

Against these the Ministry of Agriculture's Dig for Victory Leaflet,[1] No. 8, recommends Harbinger, Earliest of All (5·93), Potentate (5·82). Stonor's Exhibition and Stonor's Prolific (not listed in the John Innes Trial). Trials in the colder North

[1] The *Dig for Victory* Leaflet is obtainable from the Ministry of Agriculture, Hotel Lindum, St. Annes-on-Sea, post free.

Midlands in Nottingham show that of all the varieties named, Potentate and Market King have, over a period of years, consistently given the best and earliest crops. So, leaving you to make your own selection, we had better move on to the nicer points of cultivation.

Raising Plants from Seed.

Heat is useful for raising tomato plants since it avoids the checks to growth which fluctuating weather change bring to cold frames. The correct temperature for germinating the seed is 70° F.; once the plants are well up this should be reduced to 65° F., and that temperature maintained until the plants are ready to go out of doors. If a cold frame must be used for raising plants it is useless to sow seed earlier than April. Seed sown earlier will eventually come through, but a definite temperature is essential to germination and until that comes along the seed will stay put. At night the frame should be covered over with sacks or mats to reduce the check of night cold as much as possible. The aim is to produce a strong robust plant as different as possible to those overcrowded, drawn up, spindly, yellow-leaved cripples so often on sale on market stalls.

Soil for Seed Boxes.

The John Innes people, some time ago, went very thoroughly into the subject of standardised composts for seed growing and potting, a piece of research which will earn for them the undying gratitude of all keen gardeners.[1] They also devised some useful and easily prepared prescriptions for manures. In the trials which were mentioned earlier they used for tomato seed a mixture of 2 parts by bulk sterilised loam, 1 part peat and 1 part sand. With this was incorporated $1\frac{1}{2}$ oz. of Superphosphate and $\frac{3}{4}$ oz. of Chalk per bushel of the compost. Seed was sown on April 4, 1941, presumably in a warm house, for, by April 15-16, the seedlings were ready to be pricked out into boxes, transplanted into 3-in. pots on May 1-3, and finally planted out in the open May 29-30.

[1] Really useful leaflets published by the John Innes Institution, 31, Mostyn Road, Merton, London, S.W.19, are *Composts and Soil Sterilisation* (Nos. 1 and 2); *The John Innes Soil Steriliser* (No. 5) for the large-scale grower, and *Growing Tomatoes Out of Doors* (No. 5). All are sixpence apiece, post free, Nos. 1 and 2 being counted as a single leaflet.

The soil used for pricking out the seedlings, and for potting them later, consisted of 7 parts by bulk loam, 3 of peat and 2 of sand, with ¼ lb. per bushel J. I. Base Manure and ¾ oz. of Chalk per bushel. The J. I. Base Manure consists of 2 parts by weight Hoof and Horn, ⅛-in. grist (13 per cent Nitrogen), 2 parts Superphosphate (16 per cent Phosphoric Acid) and 1 part Sulphate of Potash (48 per cent pure Potash).

The loam used in these composts is sifted first and then sterilised, the simplest way to do this being by means of steam. Their recommendation is "to put half an inch of water in a saucepan, fill with the dry sifted earth and put the lid on; then bring to the boil and simmer for fifteen minutes. For larger quantities the soil may be suspended in sacking over boiling water in a domestic copper for thirty to forty minutes". Needless to say one should choose a day when the weekly wash is not in progress!

This may sound very elaborate and not worth the trouble, but anyone who has seen the result of growing seedlings in a box of sterilised soil, beside a box of unsterilised, will appreciate the return for the trouble taken. Now that things electrical are again obtainable, it is possible to buy small electric sterilisers. These are very simple to operate. A bushel of damp soil is put into a container, and a cable is plugged into the nearest power circuit. Heat is generated by the resistance of the damp soil to the passage of the electric current, and, when all the water has evaporated into steam, the circuit is broken and the steriliser switches itself off. The cost of operating it is said to be only a penny or two a bushel.

Size of Plants.

The plant is ready for its outside quarters when it is 10 ins. to 12 ins. high. Shortly before planting time it should be possible to sort out the rogues from the sound plants. The rogues are small, sturdy, compact plants with many leaves, varying in height from about two-thirds to half the size of the sound plants. It is a mistake to plant these as they are never fully productive. It seems that, when seed is saved from fruits from the two lower fruit trusses, a higher proportion of rogues results than when the upper two trusses are used for seed. To-day, with so great a demand for seed, this is likely to be disregarded by many people, but gardeners who save their own seed may be glad of the information. It is no use planting out-of-doors until cold nights have gone. May is a treacherous

month, and the first or second week of June is early enough
for planting even in the Southern half of the country. If,
however, one has no garden frame or greenhouse available,
and, like myself, is too busy or too lazy to spare the time
for raising plants, the best method is to find a really good
and reliable nurseryman, or gardener, who will grow the right
variety for you and have them ready by the beginning of June.
Plants much smaller than the size recommended will, of course,
grow perfectly well, but they will not allow one to secure the
full advantage in maturing a crop which is gained by planting
the larger plants.

Planting out.

The position for the plants should have been prepared some
weeks ahead of planting, the best method being to dig out a
trench a full spit deep. Into this trench a good dressing of
well-rotted farmyard manure is incorporated with the lower
spit, so that cultivation extends some 18 ins. down. The
trench should be as wide as it is deep. Having trodden down
the bottom of the trench it can now be filled in to within
4 ins. of the top to await planting time. About two weeks
before this is due the trench should have a good soak of water
so that the lower layer of soil and manure will not be dry
and the plants will then only need the minimum of watering-in
at planting time.

In early June the plants can be laid out along the row and
stakes driven in at 18 ins. to 2 ft. intervals. A plant is then
planted by each stake and during the first six weeks the soil can
be put back gradually into the trench, the additional depth of
4 ins. giving an increased root system which will develop along
the stem itself. Water must be given if the weather is dry, and
a mulch of well-rotted manure can be spread around, but not
touching, the stem of the plant to reduce evaporation. Once
well-established the best way to water the plants is to draw
out a hole with a hoe between the plants and fill this with
water. When it has sunk well in, the soil and mulch should
be pulled over the wet spot to prevent drying out and cracking
of the soil.

Staking the Plants.

It is essential to see that plants are securely staked, and
that, as growth proceeds, fresh ties are looking after it. Not
only is the succulent stem flabby but the weight of fruit soon
becomes considerable. Where a wall or fence is concerned

the best way to support the tomatoes is to set the plants a foot from the wall or fence and run a tight, well-secured wire along the wall, at about 3 ft. 6 ins. from soil level (Plate XVIII). The canes, or stakes, can then be sloped at an angle so that their tops meet the wire to which they are tied. A very rigid support results. When tying up plants do not forget that the stems increase in girth quickly and see that the ties are loose enough to allow for this.

There is now a bush Tomato (no relation to the author) which is dwarf and needs no staking. Where freedom from wind is to be had this should do well. Short tomatoes, headed back at the second truss, are earlier fruiting than those of four trusses (Plate XVII).

Side Shoots.

During the growing season side-shoots, as well as flower trusses, will appear, and, if left alone, a many-branched plant would result. Only one main stem is needed and all side-shoots should be pinched, or cut out, as soon as they are big enough to handle. When the fifth flower truss is formed the main shoot should be stopped at the second leaf beyond the last truss, and any further growths severely discouraged. Occasional leaves may be shortened back, or entirely removed when the fruit begins to ripen on the lower trusses, and by the end of August all the lower leaves up to the second truss should have been removed. Side-shoots are dealt with right through the growing period. When pinching out these, and when handling tomato leaves, the hands and fingers become stained with sap. The newcomer to tomato-growing will be surprised at the amount of yellow lather which will develop when the hands are washed. Some saps—daffodil and celery, for example—produce a dermatitis or skin eruption in certain people, but, so far as I know, tomato sap has no ill-effect.

Manuring.

Beneath our plants is, or should be, a useful layer of manure. In addition to giving food to the roots this should hold up a considerable amount of moisture, but unfortunately farmyard manure is not always obtainable. It is, however, possible to buy manures of a bulky type, such as hop-manure, which will give a fair humus content to the soil, and this, or garden compost, will do almost as well as the farmyard variety. It will, in any case, be worth while reinforcing the food supply during the growing season, and seedsmen, and horticulturally-minded chemists, keep ready-mixed fertilisers to suit the particular needs of the tomato. Artificial stimulus should not, however, be begun too early. The plants in the John Innes Test had their first dose on July 2, with their first watering, and it consisted of a mixed fertiliser known as the John Innes D Feed, with the analysis Nitrogen 6·8 per cent, Phosphate 1·94 per cent, and Potash 1·94 per cent. The analysis of other proprietary manures should be found on the packet, and, provided that this approximates, all will be well. Indeed, if the nitrogen happens to be a little lower on the particular brand you buy you can bring it up with an added pinch of Sulphate of Ammonia. Slight discrepancies are of no serious account.

The manuring should not begin until the second truss of fruit is swelling and weak doses should be given at frequent (say weekly) intervals rather than heroic doses occasionally. Little and often is a sound maxim here.

Fruiting.

Four trusses of fruit are as many as one can reasonably expect to ripen in a poor summer on an outdoor plant, but, if good strong plants are set out early in June, a fifth truss should be allowed as a speculation, and, if the season is unkind, it may still ripen in the house.

Once a fruit has begun to colour it can be picked and I have never been able to decide whether fruit so picked and ripened in the house is any less good than fruit allowed to ripen on the plant. Most of the fruit will snap off quite easily at the stalk joint just above the green sepals if this is pressed, and picking should be nearly over by the end of September. When the weather indicates that frosty nights are likely and there still remain some fruits, and perhaps that fifth truss unpicked, the whole of the trusses with their unripe fruits can be cut off and laid away between sheets of newspaper in boxes in a warm room, such as a kitchen, where the air is inclined to dryness. Here, provided that the fruits have reached their intended size (and all fruits are not necessarily top size), and the room temperature does not drop for long below 55° F., they will mature and colour perfectly and remain fit for use well into December, giving roughly a five-month season for this useful fruit.

Fruit in the Open Ground.

Where tomatoes are planted in rows in the open the rows

should be 3 ft. apart to allow for easy access. Four trusses are quite enough to run and the supporting stake must be a sound one. The manuring can be the same as that suggested for wall fruit, but watering is less likely to be needed unless the season is very dry. The mulch of manure, or compost, or even lawn mowings, should be used beneath the plants. Occasionally mildew may attack the plants when sun and dry air are absent, and the best preventive (it is not a remedy) is an occasional dust over with sulphur dust.

To-day it is possible for the amateur or the professional to double his tomato crop. By spraying the open blooms or even blooms which have dried up without setting, every one can be energised into setting full-sized fruits. . By spraying each truss once, as much as 14 lb. of fruit per outdoor plant has been obtained. The growth-promoting substances which make up the spray are cheap and easy to use, and can be bought at the multiple chemist's counter. Where this is done heavier stakes may be needed.

Pests and Diseases.

Provided that the soil, the site and the plant are good, pests seldom trouble the out-door tomato. Red Spider and green-fly usually defer attack until a plant has lost much of its moisture and the sap is sweet and concentrated. These conditions are generally found when watering has been neglected. When an attack does develop a Derris wash or Nicotine and Soap will look after it.

A disease which puzzled many growers has now been certified as Tobacco Mosaic, a virus disease which can be spread from the hand of the tobacco smoker or chewer. It affects both tobacco and tomato and it is wise for the smoker to wash his hands before handling tomato plants (he will not need to be reminded on this point after), and to avoid smoking while handling them. The mosaic disease is caused by a virus and stunts the plant and reduces yield.

Potato blight can be serious on tomatoes. In 1941 and again in 1946 many thousands of tons of outdoor tomatoes were ruined by blight, which swept over the potato fields and took the tomatoes in its stride. If spotted and rotting fruit is to be avoided it is necessary to take routine precautionary measures. The good potato grower will spray up to five times, the tomato grower may well follow his example, though three sprays will probably give him all the protection that he needs.

Bordeaux Mixture, the same fungicide which protects the potato, will do no injury to the tomato crop.[1]

This spray can either be made at home from Bluestone and Lime, using 1 lb. Bluestone Crystals to 1 lb. Quick Lime in 10 gallons of water, or one of several proprietary ready-made sprays containing copper can be used, some of which leave little or no visible deposit on leaf or fruit. Bordeaux Mixture will leave a very obvious blue deposit on fruit and leaf, and should be applied in July, and onwards as more leaf develops, so that a cover is maintained. The deposit can easily be wiped or washed off the fruit when picked.

Cracking.

This is not a disease but a condition, and indicates that a sudden flush of sap has proved too much for the skin to accommodate. It will usually occur when a drought spell is followed by a heavy fall of rain and is generally a sign that enough water has not been supplied to the plant regularly. If fruit is picked as soon as it begins to colour this trouble is decreased or avoided. Cracked fruit if left on the plant to colour may achieve this but usually the spores of botrytis rot, which are always floating about in the air in summer, gain admission and the crack will become affected with mould. The trouble is more likely to be met when plants are against a wall than when they are grown in the open, owing to the increased liability of soil near a wall to dry out.

Varieties.

It will probably be noticed that very few of the varieties of tomato recommended are to be found mentioned in gardening books save of comparatively recent publication. This is because large-scale out-of-door tomato growing began as a war-time emergency measure, and, with so much more interest taken in fruit supplies, substantial trials have been in progress with a view to increasing production. Old and trusted varieties, which were well enough a few years ago, have been superseded by better performers, and it would be unwise to suppose that in ten years' time some of the newcomers of to-day will not have made their bow and retired to make place for others.

[1] Two useful leaflets are No. 8 *Tomato Growing*, and No. 9 *Bordeaux Mixture*, in the "Dig for Victory" series. Both are obtainable from The Ministry of Agriculture, Hotel Lindum, St. Annes-on-Sea, post free on application.

XIV

SOME ODDMENTS

THE Barberry fruit is really a neglected by-product of a flowering shrub (*Berberis vulgaris*), which makes a sizeable bush up to 10 ft. in height. It is best grown as a member of the shrubbery or in any odd corner where its yellow flowers will suggest a little sunshine in spring. The Barberry can be grown from seed or from suckers, and, if flower and fruit is sought, it should be grown on a leg rather than from a stool. The berries are not useful for dessert but are said to make a very good jelly.

The Cranberry.

There is a wild cranberry but the modern public is more used to the imported Cape Cod Cranberry. A few nurserymen, specialising in unusual fruits, can supply plants of these improved strains. Once secured, stock can be increased by division of the plants in autumn, and if a piece of derelict boggy ground is available, lime-free and inclined to acidity or peaty formation, it can be made productive by planting to cranberries. Even land which is addicted to flooding, or is normally waterlogged by nearness to a sluggish stream, will grow them, and since they do not flower until June crops are not subject to frost damage. Around Christmas, 1946, the imported cranberries were on sale retail at 7s. 6d. a pound. If growing this berry do not expect more than 1s. a pound.

The Cape Gooseberry,

The true variety, *Physalis edulis*, which is beloved by South African housewives, does not appreciate the English climate. A first cousin, *Physalis ixiocarpa*, grows well in the open from seed under treatment similar to that given to the tomato. The berries within the lanterns (*Physalis francheti*, which produces the familiar red Chinese lanterns, is well known to most people) are a good size and will keep sound for as long as a year. While useless as dessert, the berries make a delicately-flavoured jelly or jam or may be stewed and eaten.

Melons.

I have never grown a melon, but no book on soft fruits would be complete without mention of the melon. Since outdoor fruits alone are to be considered, here is an account by a young market gardener, which, with permission of the author and the editor, I have filched from the Spring, 1942, issue of the *Countryman*. This seems to me a straight-forward and excellent account of melon growing, dispensing, as it does, with hot-beds and all the paraphernalia of the professional gardener. Whether you will succeed in getting "Tiger" strain without going to the Evesham district is, however, a little doubtful.

"This is how I have grown melons in cold frames for the first time. After we had dug in well-rotted stable manure, I visited my friend, the Dutch glasshouse man, who had a noble array of melon plants, and took delivery of sixty-two at the end of May. We knocked them out of their pots after previous watering, planted firmly with their soil in holes dusted with a balanced fertilizer and watered in. Watered again every week, they made rapid growth. When I came to stop them I was confronted with a maze of vines, which I sorted out to the shape of an X. I tried to set a melon at each corner, i.e. four per plant, but owing to the dull August I averaged just over two per plant. I had to de-side-shoot twice more. In mid-September the melons started to ripen—you tell by the delightful aroma, a slight crack round the stem, and the change of colour from green to yellow. The flesh is pink and of a beautiful flavour and sweetness. I chose the best melon from the most prolific plant, waited till it was perfectly ripe, ate it (not quite all myself) and then washed and dried the seed—enough for eighty lights this year, and a few for the head gardener I shall try to cajole into propagating the plants, for I have no heated glasshouse. Finally—demand Tiger strain. It is self-fertile as well as robust."

I am told by a friend who grows them that various small red-fleshed melons are easily grown in the cold house. He plants at ground level and trains up canes. It seems that all the flowers on a plant should be hand-pollinated on the same day. In 1944 I was interested to see a Russian news reel film. It showed an old woman who longed for melons but lived in so poor and arid a region that only pumpkins would grow. So she raised young pumpkin plants, split them when but a few inches high and grafted them with melon cuttings taken from

F

seedlings of the same size and age. She thus had a melon top and a pumpkin root which functioned admirably and gave fine, easily-grown crops of melons. I got a clever friend to try this out, but every graft became infected with fungus trouble. Someone who reads this may be luckier.

The Mulberry.

The mulberry, as a fruit, is enjoyed by some people, but it is unlikely that it could become popular even in wartime. An old mulberry tree, set on a perfect lawn, its trunk stained with many-coloured lichens and with its far-reaching branches propped against their breakage, is an heirloom, a thing of beauty and almost a joy for ever (a mulberry tree at Sion House of over four hundred years of age being mentioned in a book published some seventy-five years ago). It is also a sensible tree, for its flowers seem in some uncanny way to hold back their opening till all risk of frost is gone.

Of late years there has been a modest demand for mulberry leaves for feeding home-raised silk worms. Italy and France, of course, grow this tree by the hundred thousand for that purpose, but with the artificial silk industry what it is the demand for leaves is unlikely to go up. There is a paper mulberry growing as a shrub from Burma to Japan and famed through the East Indies as a source not only of paper but of the Tapa-cloth woven by the South Sea islanders. The largest tree of the mulberry species is the Red Mulberry growing in Canada to a height of 50 ft., but of no great value from a fruit point of view.

Site.

The ideal site for the mulberry in this country is a sheltered garden and while its soil requirements are not critical a warm deep soil which is well-drained is the one to ensure longevity. For choice dessert pot culture with generous manuring or wall culture is recommended but the average amateur will scarcely wish to give space to this fruit.

Planting.

Old hands tell me that February is the ideal month to plant or transplant the mulberry. Exposure of the roots to drying out should be reduced to a minimum. October and November planting are usually advised.

Propagation.

The mulberry though a slow grower is said to be easy to propagate. It is generally stated that cuttings can be taken in spring, selecting well-ripened shoots of the previous year's wood with one or two joints of two-year-old wood at the base. Autumn cuttings can also be made on the same lines. A friend writes to say that the only cuttings which can be rooted easily are those taken from the top of the tree. Layers can be made from suckers or branches or good-sized branches can be cut off, the lower end buried fairly deeply and firmly rammed and staked. From observations during the past two years I would suggest that the mulberry is not an easy subject to strike and success will reflect some credit on the gardener.

When planted as a standard tree the mulberry requires no pruning beyond thinning out branches to gain the required shape. If grown on grass young trees soon begin to bear fruit and this can be allowed to fall as it ripens. Birds usually take or spoil a good deal of it.

Pests and Diseases.

No pests or fungus troubles bother the mulberry. John Evelyn, the authority of Pepys' day, in his *Sylva* says: "It suffers no kind of vermin to breed on it, whether standing or felled, nor dares any caterpillar attack it save the silkworm only." Evelyn writes at length on the subject of raising mulberry trees from the seeds and foresaw the day when young English ladies would make pin money galore by raising mulberry leaves for silkworms and replacing the imports from France and the Orient.

Varieties.

The usual variety offered by nurserymen is the black mulberry (*Morus niger*) and this seems to be the only one cultivated for its fruit in the open in England.

The white mulberry (*Morus alba*) can be grown, and this is the variety preferred both by the silkworms and their raisers.

The Passion Fruit.

This is usually classed as a greenhouse or tropical plant, but I have had two specimens of *Passiflora incarnata* against an outside, south wall which had grown for a number of years and only perished in the cruel winter of 1939 for lack of protection, and another in February, 1947, and it is hardy enough to include among out-door soft fruits. The flower of this variety is white with a purple band and the fruit is orange-yellow, about the size of a hen's egg when well-grown. Both are very attractive and it is thrilling for the bee-lover to see the bees standing two deep in the blossom (I have counted ten in a single flower), sipping the nectar (Plate XVI).

The plants grow like a vine and the main leading shoots, which are trained along wires stretched horizontally across the wall, are allowed to grow a few feet every year, the side shoots being cut hard back, as in a vine, in early spring. Growth is extremely rapid and during the latter half of the summer flowers and fruit are produced freely and simultaneously.

Passion fruit plants can be raised from seed sown under glass or cuttings can be taken in April and rooted in sand in a frame. The flower, from which the genus derived the name, is of curiously mechanical design and one is supposed to be able to trace the crown of thorns, the nails or wounds, and the ten apostles, Peter and Judas being purposely omitted as the least worthy. The fruit consists of a thin, orange-coloured outer rind, with a soft, cottony-white interior in the middle of which reposes a succulent-looking raspberry. The flavour is very delicate. The two vines which I had carried up to two hundred fruits in a season and they were quite small plants.

The cultivation of the Passion fruit is simple and its soil requirements present few difficulties. It will succeed admirably on a medium loam and enjoys a mulch of old manure and plenty of water when in fruit. In cold districts, even in the South of England, a strawed hurdle, or some spruce branches, should be used to protect it during the winter.

For those with ambitions and a warm greenhouse there is Passiflora macrocarpa, which provides fruits as big as a medium-sized melon. Another, Passiflora edulis, yields purple fruits, while Passiflora malformis is like a golden apple.

Pyrus Japonica, which is often grown as a wall tree, is the common quince of Japan (dwarf pears are grafted on the Angers Quince, of French origin) and is valued for its scarlet, orange or white flowers. One is often asked whether the green fruits, which look and smell quite good, are fit to eat. On this point opinions differ. Some hold that while not poisonous, they cannot be classed as dessert fruit and make poor jam. Others say that if properly ripe they make excellent jelly. The variety Cydonia maulei, with orange flowers and yellow fruit, make good jam, rather of the same flavour as quince. The longest fruited variety is known as Chaenomales Cathayensis.

XV

NUTS: COB NUTS, FILBERTS AND WALNUTS

ANYONE who is fond of pruning should enjoy growing Cob Nuts and Filberts, for to make and maintain a nut tree of the correct goblet shape requires more pruning than a row of cordon apples. A nut which is well pruned and looked after will, by the time it is a hundred years old, be up to 15 ft. or 18 ft. across the top but no more than 6 ft. high. Long before this stage is reached, however, nuts will have ceased to interest you. Still, the well-trained nut plantation, in full bloom against the February sun, is a very pretty sight, as the motorist traversing Kent, who drives at a speed which will allow him to keep one eye on the road and the other over the hedge, will readily admit.

Nuts of the Cob and Filbert variety are European in origin, our hedgerow hazel being of the same species. The Filbert— the name being a shortening or corruption of "Full Beard"— found its way from Greece into Italy, thence to France and finally to England. The Cob nut is said to have come from Constantinople to this country in the reign of Charles the Second, though history goes to show that the monarch himself preferred oranges to nuts.

Propagation.

Where one buys nut trees in bulk or begs a few from a friend they are usually suckers, dug from the base of an established, but ill-trained, nut bush. Such suckers can be planted out in late autumn and then cut down to 18 ins. or so from the ground. They should then remain where they are for two years, when they will be ready to move to permanent quarters. Another method of raising nuts is to layer two-year-old shoots in October–November. Roots will form from the part below soil and the layered shoot can be removed the following autumn and treated as a sucker. October and November are the best months for planting.

Soil and Site.

A light to medium stony soil, with a well-drained but holding

sub-soil, suits the nuts. The Kentish ragstone formation is
eminently suitable, and I have seen nuts growing well among
the slab rock of the Cotswold oolitic-limestone over clay.
Shelter from the North and East winds should be provided
either by planting on a South slope or, where nuts are grown
on any considerable scale, by planting shelter belts. Shelter
is needed in February when the catkins are in blossom so that
pollenisation is aided, and in gardens a suitable corner for a
nut or two is not usually difficult to find.

Manuring.

Large, well-filled nuts are produced only on tended bushes.
When a few bushes are grown in a kitchen garden where
manure is given to neighbouring vegetables little or no
stimulation is needed in early years. Once well-established
and in bearing a mulch of well-rotted manure or compost and
a handful of bone meal will keep them thrifty and productive.

Pruning.

As mentioned before, the cup- or goblet-shaped nut-bush
takes a deal of pruning even when the desired shape is achieved.
To start training a sucker it is first cut down to about 18 ins.
from soil level. The top buds will then break into growth
and form shoots. These may be reduced to three, evenly
disposed around the central axis. The three shoots are made
into six the following season by cutting them back to buds
which are opposed and on the outer side of each branch. If
an intermediate bud indicates that one of the three top buds,
left after cutting back, will grow in the wrong direction, this
bud can be nicked off with the finger-nail when pruning. In
the autumn following the six shoots are again cut back,
doubling them to twelve, which is the required number of
leaders to form the bush. These are headed back annually
until they have reached the required height, while all side
shoots are spurred in to produce thin tough growths upon
which the fruit will be carried.

In the young tree, once the shape is established and catkins
begin to form in February, no pruning should be done until
these male flowers have finished shedding their pollen on to
the little crimson tufts which are the female flowers and will
form the nuts. When, on a sunny day, pollen can no longer
be shaken off in clouds, pruning can be begun. Side shoots

are cut back to the fifth leaf bud, and the leader or main branch
is shortened according to its strength as compared with its
fellows; a strong extension being reduced by from one-half to
two-thirds of its length, always cutting to a bud pointing in
the desired direction for continuation growth. Twiggy side
shoots will provide bearing wood, strong growths will not
and should at all times be cut out or cut back hard. Summer
pruning of the side shoots, which is practised as a further check
to growth, consists in bending and twisting side shoots so that
they break but remain hanging, the point of the break being
a hand's breadth from the main branch. These broken shoots
are left to hang, the idea being to increase sap loss and so
reduce the tendency to form fresh growth which a clean cut
would encourage. These broken shoots are cut off in the
winter pruning.

Winter pruning consists in cutting off the broken shoots and
thinning out the old wood, which has borne nuts in the current
season, so that a constant replacement of new, twiggy wood is
secured. Strong growths, arising from the centre or other
parts of the bush, which are additional to the main leader
shoots, are not wanted and should be cut out. Suckers, which
may spring from the ground beside the stem, are best twisted
out rather than cut to discourage basal buds from breaking
into growth.

Where close pruning is altogether too much trouble nuts
can still be grown by a compromise between attention and
neglect. The bushes will not produce such fine nuts or such
big and regular crops. The method is to allow the bush to
follow its own inclinations as to growth but to keep the centre
open and to keep sucker growths removed.

Picking and Storage.

Even when the port is not conspicuous by its absence few
things are more disappointing at the dessert stage than mouldy
nuts. To avoid this embarrassment nuts should be left to
ripen to their full brown upon the bush, or even allowed to
ripen so that they fall. I realise that, with the grey squirrel
infiltrating into every coppice, this latter proviso is a little
optimistic. Suppose we say that for keeping quality one must
have a fully ripe nut and that after collection it must be quite
dry before being put away in storage? When the shell is
really dry, after a few days on the attic floor, guarded by a
trusty cat or a barrage of mouse-traps, the nuts can be packed

away in boxes, tins or any other receptacle, using either salt
or dry sand over each layer.

Varieties.

The following are the best varieties of Cob and Filbert and
those marked with an asterisk have the special commendation
of the late Mr. E. A. Bunyard and Mr. N. B. Bagenal, both
excellent judges and of great experience.

COBNUTS.

Cosford Cob: Round nuts. Thin-shelled and borne in
clusters of six. Of good flavour and a free cropper.

Kentish Cob or *Lambert's Filbert:* The best cobnut for
general culture. Nuts very large. Very hardy and succeeds
anywhere. It is the most popular Kent market variety.

Pearson's Prolific: Medium size. Thin shell and a regular
cropper. I am told by a wise friend that this variety should
always be included because of its high value as a pollinator.

FILBERTS.

The White Filbert: Nuts white, oval, small but of very good
flavour. A shy bearer which needs a warm site.

The Red Filbert: The same qualities as the White Filbert
but the nut has a red skin.

Prolific: The largest and earliest. A good bearer.

Pests.

Nuts have a formidable list of pests. Over a dozen varieties of
caterpillar infest them, but most prominent among them are the
following: The Winter Moth, whose green caterpillars progress
by looping their bodies. This habit distinguishes them from
the Tortrix Caterpillars, which may vary in tint from green to
buff and dark brown, but are shy and wriggle hastily backwards
when alarmed or touched.

Winter Moth caterpillars hatch out during March and April,
and owing to their small size are often unnoticed until they
have attained some size and achieved much damage to buds
and opening leaf. The only method of protection is the early
application of Arsenate of Lead wash, using the recommended
dilution of $\frac{1}{2}$ lb. of the dry powder form in 25 gallons of
water. Where caterpillars are prevalent several applications
can be usefully employed from April till the end of June.

The Nut Weevil can be a very damaging pest, the female

boring into the nutlets in May to lay her eggs. The maggot, having emerged, completes its first stage of development inside the nut and leaves through the original hole, falling to the ground between July and August. Once down it enters the soil, pupates and appears in the following spring ready to carry on mama's evil work. As may be imagined, this weevil is no easy pest to control, though, to some extent, the June spray of Arsenate is effective since it poisons the food of the feeding weevils which eat the leaf, thus reducing the weevil population. D.D.T. dust is now said to be even better applied early in June.

Aphis is another pest of the nut family but this can easily be prevented by a 5-per-cent strength Tar-oil wash in December, not forgetting that the blossom period for nuts begins January–February and allows little latitude for postponement. Where an aphis attack develops in summer it can be dealt with by using the standard Nicotine and Soap (or wetting agent) spray.

Big-Bud Mite, of the same family as the mite which attacks black currant buds, affects the nut tree but in the case of this fruit blind buds are formed. Infection of the currant by the nut mite does not take place. Where the attack is definitely severe the treatment as recommended for black currant Big-Bud Mite will be found effective.

Walnuts.

In peacetime great quantities of walnuts are imported from the Continent, the long sacks of Grenoble Nuts being a feature of the Covent Garden Christmas market. The commoner types of walnut, small and thick-shelled, have spread across Europe from Persia and Asia, while eastwards, in Kashmir and Afghanistan, a large, thin-shelled type has been developed and is preferred. Many of our English walnuts are seedlings of no known parentage and, in too many cases, of poor performance. The profitable production of walnuts can only be undertaken when grafted trees are planted.

It is not generally known that sugar can be extracted from the sap of the walnut tree in the same way that maple sugar is obtained. Some years ago, on a sunny morning in May, following a severe frost which shrivelled every leaf and shoot of a nice young walnut tree in my garden, I cut a twig which was no thicker than a pencil to see how far the frost had killed the shoot back into the wood. Passing the spot later in the day I noticed a pool of sap beneath the end of the cut twig, and sap steadily dripping from the cut. For curiosity I tied a string to the twig so that the drops of sap were guided down into a bucket. In four or five days more than a gallon of sap had collected. Sugar was, at that time, easily obtainable from the grocer, but, had I cared to boil that sap down to a suitable consistency, a syrup which would crystallize out into sugar of a sort should theoretically have been obtainable.

Anyone wishing to make the experiment may be confirmed in their research by the following extracts from the 1911 edition of *The Encyclopædia Britannica*, thus leaving me blameless for unexpected results.

Under Walnut: "Sugar is also prepared from the sap in a similar manner to that obtained from the maples." Under Maple: "Sugar is principally extracted from this species (*Acer rubrum*), the sap being boiled and the syrup when reduced to a proper consistence runs into moulds to form cakes. Trees growing in low and moist situations afford the most sap but the least sugar. A cold N.W. wind with frosty nights and sunny days in alternation, tends to incite the flow which is more abundant during the day than the night. A thawing night is said to promote the flow and it ceases during a S.W. wind; and so sensitive are the trees to aspect and climatic variations that the flow of sap on the South and East side has been noticed to be earlier than on the North and West side of the same tree. The average quantity of sap per tree is from 12 to 24 gallons in a season."

Since frosty nights and sunny days are infrequent in our climate your opportunity of getting one up on the Excise Department is limited, but it will be seen from these extracts that the walnut tree may be induced to part with more than nuts, and for those with large trees in frosty situations which seldom mature a crop, a little sugar rendering may provide interest and profit.[1]

Site for Planting.

Provided that a soil is well-drained and will grow apple

[1] Since the first edition a friend tried this and writes: "I drew a bucket of juice and evaporated it to an egg-cup full. It was intensely salt and not at all sweet. The answer is, of course, this was the ascending sap laden with nutrient solutions from the soil. The descending sap, after elaboration by the leaves, should supply sugar, but this must be drawn from the bark of the tree and not from the sap-wood beneath." *Experientia docet.*

trees it will grow walnut trees. When young, walnut trees are very susceptible to frost damage, and if small, newly-grafted specimens are planted they must be covered during radiation frost nights in April and May or the growing tips will be badly frosted. For this reason every effort should be made when a site for a walnut tree is chosen to select one which is well up out of the valley bottom. Where well-sited walnuts of the right sorts are planted they can be extremely profitable both as regards nuts and for their timber which is always in demand.

As with Cob nuts and Filberts shelter from North and East wind is desirable, since the walnut bears its own catkins early in spring and warmth is helpful for pollination. The pollen is wind-borne from the male catkins, and in some cases the female nutkins are not advanced enough in development to utilise this, so instead of swelling the nutlets will drop off. The difference in development between the flower and the nutlet may cease later in the life of the tree, but, in order that the season of fertilisation be extended, it is always advisable to plant another walnut of a different variety as a neighbour.

Propagation.

Walnuts grown from nuts do not come true, and even where a nut from an immensely productive tree has been grown there is no guarantee that as good a walnut will result, though quite good nuts may be forthcoming in from ten to twelve years' time. The only safe tree to plant is the grafted tree, and walnut-grafting is no operation for the average amateur. The best tree to buy is a young established walnut of three to four years old. October is the best month to plant and also in which to prune, or rather remove unwanted shoots, for beyond thinning out to shape in early years no pruning is needed.

Planting Distance.

Walnuts of great age make very large trees but such are the exception rather than the rule, and 40 ft. to 50 ft. apart is enough room to allow.

Pests.

Beneath the floorboards of a small farmhouse attic, an electrician busy laying wiring once showed me how the spaces between the joists were packed almost solid with thousands of age-blackened walnut shells. The nearest tree to the house was a full hundred yards away, so the mice had quite a long trek carrying their walnuts. Indeed, it was rather a surprising feat on the part of the mice, since it meant that each nut must be pushed and rolled along or be clasped to the bosom of a mouse while it lay upon its back and was pulled along by the tail over a hundred yards of grass and gravel, with heaven knows what shifts ahead when stairs or hollow walls had to be negotiated. Mice, squirrels, rooks and jackdaws are among the major pests of the walnut. Aphis may attack young shoots in their early stages, but, apart from that, the aromatic and astringent juices of the walnut appear to deter insect invaders.

There are certain bacterial blights and leaf spottings which are active in wet years like 1946, but these rarely call for remedial measures, and they and the occasional insect pests are mainly met with in the nursery days of the young tree.

Gathering and Storing Walnuts.

Never having beaten my wife I am unable to support the old adage

> "A woman, a dog and a walnut tree,
> The more you beat 'em the better they be."

but it is only right to say that the walnut tree is beaten purely for convenience and not for pleasure.

Walnuts are gathered green or ripe. Those for pickling should be taken in early to late July with the green skin still around them. Nuts from the "June Drop," which generally comes in July, make good pickle. Where full-grown nuts are pickled it is better to treat each tree's nuts separately as pickling quality varies considerably. Nuts for storage, if they are to keep—and there is considerable variation in the keeping qualities of different varieties—must reach full ripeness and fall by October. If you have a high local mouse and squirrel population this may not be allowed and the tall ladder, the long pole and the beating must be employed. Such nuts, having not fallen naturally, are apt to be slightly immature and can be kept spread out in a dry shed for a few days prior to husking.

The complete removal of all husk and shred is important, for, if left on, the material forms the suitable site for mould to begin and many nuts are lost by this omission. After all the husk has been removed the final cleaning process can be done, using a brush and a pan of water. Another method of cleaning nuts is to scrub them in a tub with sand and water and a stiff broom before drying as before. The nuts can then be rough-dried and spread out to complete drying in some warm and airy place. The ideal method is to spread on wire trays and dry in a draught. Once dry they may be stored in sand. Some prefer to sprinkle salt on the nuts as each layer is sanded over. If kept too long in a dry atmosphere there is a tendency for the kernels to shrivel and the addition of salt to the sand helps to retain a moderate moisture content. Where nuts have been damaged by birds or squirrels the best plan is to shell and dice them without delay.

Varieties.

The most extensive investigation in this country into walnut culture has been carried out by East Malling Research Station and their recommendations include two varieties of English walnuts for pickling in July, namely Leeds Castle and Patching, both of which grow in clusters. They also recommend the following, which are numbered but not named; they are East Malling 95, 162, 202, 589, 719. These are all varieties which are late enough to miss most frosts.

Good French types, which are on offer from nurserymen, are Franquette and Mayette, Freyne and Melyanaise and Parisienne. The latter can generally be bought on steps up to 4 ft. and 5 ft. high; high enough to escape ground frosts on good sites.

The Sweet or Spanish Chestnut has been omitted from the nuts, since it is really a timber tree and best planted for the production of stakes, the wood having excellent lasting powers when buried in the soil. In the Southern half of the country nut crops can be had, but the nuts are usually small and often fail to ripen. Grown as coppices for cutting at intervals of every so many years the Spanish chestnut can be a very useful proposition, as anyone who has bought large numbers of stakes for fruit tree supports will realise.

Some fine large chestnuts were shown at the R.H.S. Show in London on October 16th, 1945, which came from the Marquis Camden's estate at Bayham Abbey. A friend in Herts. tells me that a large fruited variety called "Maron de Lyon" is also available from nurseries.

XVI

IS SPRAYING NECESSARY?

BEFORE answering this question let us review the fruit position of 1941. Fruit was consistently scarce and very dear. The gooseberry crop was not large, for frost played havoc with the young berries. It did the same in 1944 and again in 1945. In private gardens bullfinches, tits and sparrows enjoyed their usual diet of vitamins, composed largely of fruit buds. Mildew in summer was rampant on the gooseberries which had survived the combined assaults of low temperature and birds. Here and there Gooseberry Sawfly caterpillars defoliated whole bushes, destroying any chance of a useful crop.

Black currants, too, were few and far between, for they also hate cold nights in May, and Greenfly and Big-bud took their usual rations of growth and bud. In many a garden the raspberries and loganberries promised well but, when the time came to pick them, a large proportion were housing the little wriggling grubs of the Raspberry Beetle.

These are but a few of the usual attacks which reduce our first crop and, with the exception of the bullfinches and the frost, all could have been prevented or reduced by the use of the appropriate spray or dust applied at the right time. Surely at present prices pest control is a fine investment?

To some amateurs (and their number decreases yearly) spraying is a "shot in the dark", and if a successful control results the achievement will be almost as surprising as the production of rabbits from the conjurer's hat. The real thrill of merited success is reserved for those who know the whys and wherefores of spray application, whose shots are aimed and who consistently score a bull.

One can divide insect pests roughly into two classes—sapsuckers and those which bite, nibble or eat leaf, blossom and fruit. In the first class come the Aphis, plain and woolly, Capsid Bugs, Red Spider and the Scale insects. In the second class come all the Caterpillars, Fruit Weevils and Beetles, the apple and plum Sawflies, Pear Midge, Plum Fruit Moth caterpillars, Codlin Moth and such vermin—quite a considerable collection.

There are, of course, other pests such as Bud Mite which makes the big buds on black currants, Shot-hole Borers, Currant Clearwing and Leopard Moth caterpillars, which attack the solid wood or tunnel up the pithy centres of branches. These latter are in the minority and some are very hard to attack or control. Quite a number of the main insect pests only make occasional appearances on soft fruit in the garden and need be attacked only when they do appear. Others are always present and may demand egg-killing or protective applications as a matter of routine hygiene.

The approach to controlling any pest must, when possible, be begun during the over-wintering egg stage. Certain pests, notably Aphis and Apple-sucker, are completely controllable at this stage where their eggs happen to be laid on the several varieties of fruit tree or bush which they afflict.

Once hatched from the eggs, the sucking insects, which extract sap from leaf or shoot, must be attacked by a contact wash which poisons them via the breathing apparatus, as when soap and nicotine are used, or by paralysing the nervous or breathing system where nicotine is replaced by Derris. Derris, while paralytic to the cold-blooded insects, is non-poisonous to warm-blooded creatures, and so is an extremely valuable wash for all horticultural purposes where insect pests are concerned. D.D.T. is, like Derris, a selective poison, killing some pests and sparing others.

Biting insects, such as caterpillars and some leaf-eating weevils, require a different approach, and since their food supply includes the external covering of leaf or fruit a coating of Arsenate of Lead can be sprayed on the leaf before they begin to eat it. Arsenic, being cheap and a cumulative poison, has proved itself to be a stand-by for the commercial fruit-grower but, being a poison, it can only be bought by the amateur when it has been signed for in the poison book which every chemist keeps. Once on the leaf a fatal dose is soon absorbed by the pest and death takes place save in a few instances. Apple blossom weevils, which emerge from those tight, brown apple-blossom buds which failed to open to pink-and-white, feed mainly on young apple leaves and evade the issue by ejecting the outer layer of the leaf and enjoying the inner tissues, but to-day are easily controlled with D.D.T. spray or dust just about the egg-laying stage. Codlin Moth caterpillars, which bore into the apple soon after hatch, eat so little skin that if the coating of poison is to be toxic it must be adequate or renewed at intervals if any control is to be expected. The Sawfly caterpillar (not to be confused with the Gooseberry Sawfly) which attacks the apple should be controlled at hatchibg-time, and the nicotine which is applied when the blossoms have just fallen should kill it by the time it has just finished enjoying its very first little meal.

Roughly then, pest control on soft fruits boils down to Nicotine or Derris for the sucking insects and Arsenate of Lead, D.D.T. or Derris for most of the biting insects. Both Arsenate of Lead and Nicotine are deadly poisons, but the former remains poisonous as long as it stays as a coating on the leaf or fruit, while Nicotine vaporises rapidly and kills only over a period of minutes or hours, depending on how hot or cool the day may happen to be. Derris has a life of several days and D.D.T. of several weeks, and during that time will affect any susceptible insect coming into contact with it. Because Arsenate of Lead is persistently poisonous it must not be applied to a fruit within two months or so of picking time, while Nicotine and Derris may be used, if necessary, a few days before the fruit is eaten without fear of ill-effects or flavour.

Half the battle is won if spraying is begun early in the attack. When Aphis is developing on fruit tree shoots and leaves the normal reaction on the part of the leaf is to curl up. One sees the tops of black currant shoots cease growth and bunch up when the Aphis attack is well established and the pest is then hard to get at. In an early summer attack by Aphis, plum leaves roll up tightly, shrivel to brown and die. Apple leaves curl over and shoots become stunted and twisted, while such apples as may be present never grow to any size and are useless. The particular Aphis which normally attacks the red currant raises a red blister on the leaf on the under side of which only a few Aphis are to be seen. Mealy Plum Aphis, on the other hand, coming, as it does, when leaf is fully mature, does not curl up the leaf, although the whole underside may be a grey felty mass of these disgusting Aphids. Fruit leaves do not all react in the same way, but in every case a bad attack can be avoided provided that early indications of trouble are followed by a thorough spraying. Once the infestation is fully developed it is often almost impossible to get at it, and not only is the crop lost but next year's is also affected.

To be effective a contact spray must be aimed. To wet the

visible tops of the leaves is not enough, since many pests develop beneath the leaf where they are out of the wet and not easy to see. The Big-Bud Mite of the black currant is on the move when the bud has opened and only then can it be attacked. Red Spider is mostly below the leaf, and if sprayed for, one must be sure to wet the underside of every leaf, for this pest may run through a considerable number of generations in a good summer and quite a small nucleus will develop to astronomic proportions in a few weeks by compound multiplication. Provided the underneath of the leaves is wetted you can be quite sure that the upper surfaces will get their share.

This is less important in a cover spray such as Arsenate of Lead, though the poison will remain longer on the lower side of the leaf than on the upper surface. When a Lime-Sulphur wash is being used to prevent apple scab a good medium spray should be applied, and when the tree begins to drip there is not much point in putting more wash on. Once applied, Sulphur is a very active protector since its invisible particles "explode" in all directions in bright sunlight, while in solution in raindrops it is splashed a yard or more in every direction during a rainstorm. It is this activity and ubiquity which makes it difficult for the wandering spores of scab fungus to find a congenial resting-place on a sprayed leaf in which to put out roots and spread.

For the convenience or curiosity of those readers who are interested in pest control I have extracted the spraying programmes for the various fruits from the full list as published in *Tree Fruit Growing*, Vol. I. and II. At first sight these look very formidable but you will notice that in the table dealing with black currants, for example, there is one spray in capital letters. For this fruit this is the only essential spray. The others may or may not be needed. The programme for gooseberries is more extensive, but here again unless your gooseberries or any other fruit are obviously in need of spraying for specific troubles there is no need to apply them.

The spraying tables are approximately correct for the southern half of the country. Applications for the northern half will be later. In a year like 1945, where winter extends right through January and beyond, the spraying date may be considerably extended but one must not delay longer than one need, for once the temperature rises buds make up for lost time and develop fast. Try then to spray in winter as early as possible and do not leave it hopefully to the latest date suggested.

Once the amateur has begun to realise the nature of the attack by the insect or fungus and the reasons for the particular method of combating it, spraying becomes extremely interesting. For those who wish to develop such an interest the Ministry of Agriculture is glad to foster it by sending appropriate leaflets giving the life history of the pest and all manner of useful information on control. For the convenience of readers I append a list.

SOFT FRUITS—BLACK CURRANT (RED AND WHITE CURRANTS No. 1 SPRAY ONLY)

	Stage	Approximate date of Spraying—South and Midlands	Materials per 50 galls. of water	Pests and Diseases controlled
1.	DORMANT	Dec. to Feb.	3½ galls. tar-oil emulsion or	Aphis
	DORMANT	Mid-Feb.	3¼ galls. D.N.C. petroleum oil emulsion	Aphis, capsid, winter moth caterpillars
2.	Flower-buds still a tight cluster but flowers not opened	Early April	1 gall. lime-sulphur	Big bud mite
3.	After fruit is picked	Late July into August	Bordeaux mixture made with 4 lb. copper sulphate, 6 lb. hydrated lime or Bouisol	Leaf spot Rust

GOOSEBERRY

Stage	Approximate date of Spraying—South and Midlands	Materials per 50 galls. of water	Pests and Diseases controlled
1. DORMANT or BEFORE BUD-BURST	Dec. to Feb. / Early to mid-Feb.	3½ galls. tar-oil emulsion / 3½ galls. D.N.C. petroleum oil emulsion	Aphis / Aphis, capsid, winter moth and gooseberry red spider
2. FRUIT SETTING	Late April	Sulphur dust	American mildew
3. END OF MAY	End May	½ lb. derris* / ¼ lb. wetter / ¼ gall. lime-sulphur	Sawfly (1st brood) / American mildew
4. End June	End June early July	½ lb. derris / ¼ lb. wetter	Sawfly (2nd brood)

Note that several varieties of gooseberry, notably the yellow ones are damaged by sulphur; for these one can use a spray made of 9 lb. of washing soda and 5 lb. soft soap (though few could afford it to-day) to 50 gallons of water. Few practical people, however, have much faith in this brew, it needs renewing so often. D.D.T. horticultural dusts and sprays can now be used in place of Derris. Follow the makers' instructions.

RASPBERRY, LOGAN AND BLACKBERRY

	Stage	Approximate date of Spraying—South—and Midlands	Materials per 50 galls. of water	Pests and Diseases controlled
1.	Just before bud burst	From early to mid-March	3½ galls tar-oil or D.N.C. petroleum emulsion; spray the soil as well as the cane	Raspberry moth, aphis, capsid
2.	First flowers opening	Early June	Derris or lonchocarpus dust	Larvæ of the raspberry beetle
3.	First fruits ripening	Mid to end of June	¼ lb. derris / ¼ lb. wetter or repeat the derris dusting	Larvæ of the raspberry beetle

STRAWBERRY

	Stage	Approximate date of Spraying—South—and Midlands	Materials per 50 galls. of water	Pests and Diseases controlled
1.	When crown is showing growth	March to early April	¾ gall. lime-sulphur / ¼ lb. wetter / 1¼ oz. nicotine	Strawberry aphis, red spider and mildew
2.	BEFORE FLOWER-ING	Mid-May	ditto	ditto
3.	After fruit picking or de-blossoming new plants	Mid-July to mid-August	ditto	ditto
4.	After fruit is over		ditto	ditto

NOTE: Plant only runners from certified parent plants if you wish for long-lived strawberry beds.

Advisory Leaflets.

Insect and Other Pests.	*Number of Leaflet*
*Red Spider	10
Apple Sawfly	13
Black Currant Mite (Big-bud)	27
*Gooseberry Sawfly	30
Codling Moth	42
Magpie Moth	65
Fruit Tree Capsids	154
*Raspberry Beetle	164
Woolly Aphis	187
Gooseberry Red Spider	305
Injurious Fungi.	
Apple and Pear Scab	245
Silver Lead Disease	246
*American Gooseberry Mildew	273

Note.—Any four of the Advisory Leaflets may be obtained free and post free from the Ministry of Agriculture, Hotel Lindum, St.-Annes-on-Sea, Lancs. Copies in excess of four should be purchased from H.M. Stationery Office, York House, Kingsway, London, W.C.2, or through a bookseller, price 1d. each. (2d. by post) or 9d. per dozen (11d. by post).

Those marked * are a useful four if full advantage is to be taken of the offer.

Spraying Appliances.

The barrow type of spraying machine, complete with wheels, a powerful pump and adequate strainer, is now a very expensive proposition and beyond the average gardener's pocket; we will therefore disregard it.

The bucket pump, which is double acting, so that a continuous spray can be maintained, can just be operated as a single-handed outfit, but having so used it myself I recommend it to none but strong, silent men. Provided one has an assistant to pump, and provided also that the short piece of hose is replaced by a longer section so that a wider range of action is provided, this type of machine is quite able to deal with any soft fruit spraying in an average garden.

Stirrup pumps are now languishing in vast numbers for lack of incendiary bombs, but as spraying machines they can do good work, provided one person pumps and the other sprays.

If one cares to fasten the business end on to a length of batten quite tall trees can be reached with the spray.

The Knapsack sprayer is a very effective one-man weapon, but is expensive to-day.   These can be had to pump by hand or as a cylinder which before being hoisted on to one's back is filled with wash and pumped up to the requisite pressure to discharge its contents.   Of the two I prefer the former.   It is also good exercise, particularly for the triceps muscle of the right arm, but apt to lead to unilateral development, and I commend makers to think out a machine which can be operated from either side.

There are also small, double-acting syringes which will deliver a continuous spray and are fitted with a length of hose which allows one to suck the wash from the mixing bucket.   These are useful, but their action is a little apt to be tiring, and the tendency is for the spray to be too fine.

The ordinary garden syringe of the Abol type, with a curved end so that a spray can be delivered at an angle of 45 degrees, can be a very useful weapon for fruit bush spraying in powerful hands and a surprising amount of spray can be put on in a short time with considerable force.

As for dusts, these are now so fine that they can be blown through an atomising gun of the Flit type.   The great advantage of dust over spray is speed of application and penetrative power, but these advantages only apply when almost completely calm air conditions are present.   The time to use dust is early morning or late in the evening.

Hints on Spraying[1] and Machines.

1. See that you follow the maker's directions when mixing a wash.   His ideas are sure to be best.

2. Where poisonous washes are used see that all cans and buckets are well washed out after use.   If you have a river at the bottom of the garden do not tip surplus wash into it; some fishes do not care for poisons.

3. Keep poisons such as Nicotine and Arsenate of Lead under lock and key and see that labels are intact.

4. A contact wash aimed at the insect can be a coarse drenching wash.

5. A wash designed to leave a coating of poison or fungicide

[1] For the convenience of amateurs full spraying tables for all fruits—soft and tree fruits—together with dates of application are given in both volumes of *Tree Fruit Growing* in this series.

on the leaf or fruit should be a fine spray, using no more than enough to wet the surface without an undue amount of drip.

6. Unused wash should not be kept "for next time" but should be poured into a hole in the ground or the drain. Therefore mix no more than you can easily apply.

7. For low power spraying the calm of the evening or early morning is best. Nicotine is most effective when the day is warm. For dusting calm is essential.

8. After spraying clean out the pump or syringe thoroughly. Oil the plunger rod and cup leathers before putting away. Dust guns also need cleaning and oiling periodically.

9. Hoses should be kept in a cool dark place. The best place is in a tub under water, or on bricks which stand under water on the bottom of the tub. Sunlight causes the rubber to crack and perish and rubber hose is very, very dear these days.

XVII

MUSHROOMS

MUSHROOMS can hardly be described as fruit but their war-time price raises them so far above the vegetable tribe that they stand in a class by themselves. Personally I think it is ridiculous to control the price of the choicest Cox's Orange Pippins at 1/- a pound and allow mushrooms to be offered in the same shop window as high as 15/- a pound. The explanation for this is quite obvious. There are not nearly enough mushrooms to go round. The powers that impose price controls dearly love their breakfast kidneys and mushrooms, so mushrooms are omitted in order that they may reach the high price which lack of supply and keenness of demand ensures. Only the rich can afford to buy them. The day when the country greengrocer paid his tuppence a pound for field mushrooms and retailed them at sixpence is gone for ever.

Mushrooms are curious fungi. A research worker once assured me that if mushrooms are burnt to ash by intense heat it is always possible to obtain from a quantity of them a globule of pure silver. Unlike the plant tribe this fungus (in the variety *Agaricus hortensis* as grown for market) flourishes in complete darkness and needs no light at all to complete its development. It is entirely dependent on the right medium to grow in, adequate moisture and a definite range of temperature. It is common throughout the temperate zones of Europe, and I am told that in Kenya even on the equator it grows in profusion where horses and cattle are grazed and the height of the land provides suitable temperature.

The commercially grown types of mushrooms are distinct varieties from the field mushroom, which is known as *Agaricus campestris*, and the horse mushroom, *Agaricus arvensis*. Two types are grown, a white and a brown, the former making the higher price, the latter thought by some to be more prolific.

In the field the mushroom at full maturity produces seeds or spores which fall as a black dust from the gills on the underside of the fully developed specimen when these have changed from pink to black. Such spores may fall directly on to manure which has been dropped in the field or may be eaten with the grass when the horse is grazing and deposited with the droppings well away from the original mushroom, thus spreading the crop. As the droppings decay to compost the spores are able to produce mycelium or roots and a mushroom plant comes into being. The mycelium can also remain in the soil ready to start into growth when conditions are suitable.

It seems to be established that land on which stallions are grazed is particularly prolific in mushrooms and the urine from stallions was favoured by those who produced the bricks of mushroom spawn for commercial users. To-day the compost is prepared under sterile conditions, impregnated with spawn and sold in the familiar cardboard cartons. It would seem that in this case the sex hormone may be a factor in development, though it is apparently not an essential one. When making compost the French esteem the manure from hard-worked, corn-fed horses first, followed by the manure from mules, asses, sheep, and finally the humble rabbit. The cow it seems has no place in its economy.

It is likely that the use of horse manure, which was always insisted on by the old time growers, may not be nearly so essential as was thought. It is undoubtedly the best and easiest material to compost, but one can now get composts with a straw base using 13 lb. of Nitrogen, 4 lb. of Phosphoric Acid and 10 lb. of Potash to each ton of fibrous material having a content of 70 per cent moisture. Nitrogen can be organic, as in dried blood, or inorganic, as in nitro-chalk. Phosphate can be bone meal or superphosphate, but it seems that potash is the most important constituent since its omission lowers the yield of mushrooms by as much as half.

Many mushroom growers hold that thundery weather and severe thunderstorms, when the spawn is "running" or active, will destroy the chance of a crop in beds of mushrooms planted outside. Some also hold that the flushes of the crop become heavier as the moon approaches the full, the yield declining as the moon wanes.

Although mushrooms can be grown outdoors on ridges covered with straw, under garden lights, below greenhouse staging, in boxes, or in sheds and barns, there is no doubt that the use of caves, cellars or disused railway tunnels, all of which provide an even temperature, is the better method, provided one attends to hygiene. Pests and diseases spread very rapidly in the neighbourhood of this crop and must be very rigidly controlled.

The large caves at Chislehurst, used by thousands for shelter from the various bombardments of London, were once famous for their mushrooms, but probably the vast quarries near Paris are the best known. Some of these had miles of corridors up to and over a dozen feet in height. It is said that in caves at Méry, in 1867, over twenty miles' run of mushroom beds were put down, and up to 1931, when a big tariff was imposed on imported mushrooms, as much as 600 tons a year were brought over here from France. To-day, mushroom growing is quite a big industry in our country, in spite of the shocking price usually charged for those offered for sale.

Those who begin to grow mushrooms should realise that when they see pictures showing masses of mushrooms and innumerable tiny white dots of immature buttons a vast proportion of these will never develop. The reason for this is that the threads of mycelium from which the abortive mushrooms have grown are unable to support them, with the result that a proportion of the young mushrooms dry up and die. Commercial growers of outdoor mushrooms consider that to bring 25 per cent of the visible crop to maturity is good going. It has been said, and not without some background of truth, that any fool can grow one crop of mushrooms, but after the first success troubles begin to crop up. These troubles are insects and fungous diseases, and it is absolutely vital to success that these should be controlled.

If you have read as far as this you may feel inclined to say: "My word, this fellow knows quite a bit about mushroom growing." Don't you believe it. The fact is that they have always interested me, titillated my palate and pleased my eye. I have read about them, talked to a few commercial growers, and admired their crops or consoled them in their failure, but until people asked me last year to write a chapter about how to grow them I had never bothered to do so.

In my attempts at mushroom growing in the summer of 1944 I tried to be as casual as possible, deliberately leaving undone those things which I ought to have done and then trying my best to get over the troubles which arose. It is, therefore, possible that this account may be really helpful and encouraging to beginners. Good advice will duly be forthcoming at the end of this chapter, but in the meantime let me tell you all about it.

Being inordinately fond of mushrooms and having fallen out with my neighbour in 1943 for ranging his pastures in

search of these fungi during such time as I was reputed
to be fire-watching while he was enjoying the well-deserved
sleep of an overworked farmer, I determined to plant a bed
of mushrooms for my own delectation and so avoid unjust
recriminations.

Towards the end of May I bought two cartloads of warmish
manure, mainly horse but not entirely innocent of cow manure,
and dumped it outside an empty shed which stands in our
paddock. As the building, designed in bygone days as a two-
stall loose-box, is a very flimsy wooden affair and broody hens
are imprisoned at times in the one half, my fungal activities
were confined to the other. The figure will show the layout of
the shed and the mushroom bed. The space used was 12 ft.
long by 7 ft. wide, the floor was concrete, and a space was
marked off to allow for entry and for traffic.

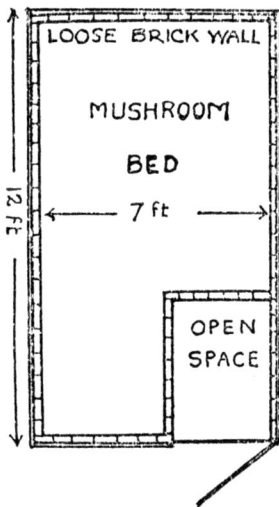

At one time the doors opening into the paddock were
complete, but to-day both top
halves have fallen to pieces and
the bottom halves of the door
are ready to do so. I therefore fixed up an old curtain to
hang across the door and
tempered interior draughts between the two halves of the
loose-box by hanging sacks
down the centre of the shed.
You will therefore realise that
I was planting in a ruin and
not in a nice draught-proof,
warm, leak-proof building. Indeed even when I had finished
patching up the roof and walls
there was still much daylight
to be seen.

Having first built a 12-inch-high wall of loose bricks
round three sides of the interior of the loose-box I wheeled
the manure in and stacked it in a sizeable heap. So far as
quality went it was quite satisfactory, being from 60 to 70
per cent of its bulk wheat straw and the remainder horse
manure with a little cow manure. It was fresh enough to
steam when it was being handled.

The instructions on the carton of mushroom spawn told me that one carton would be enough to spawn 60 sq. ft. of bed and that one ton of manure would make compost for this area. As my floor space was roughly 80 sq. ft., I had enough manure to make a compost bed a good deal thicker than was really essential.

Now came mistake number one. I disregarded the instructions about spraying the concrete bed and the shed with disinfectants and the manure with an atomised oil of pyrethrum. I decided that very few amateurs would dream of going to so much trouble.

Making the Compost.

"Even fermentation," I read, "is one of the main considerations in changing stable manure into a state suitable for mushroom growing. A number of turnings are necessary to achieve this."

My heap was about 4 ft. high, 6 ft. wide and 10 ft. long. When I had wheeled it in I had watered each barrowful well and shaken the stuff out as loosely as I could. This seemed to have been the correct treatment, for a few days later the top of the heap was damp and it was steaming gently. Seven days after being first stacked it was ready for a turn, and I found it a laborious job turning the inside of the heap to the outside and *vice versa*, since the shed was much too small to work in comfortably. I discovered that my right funny-bone still possessed a sense of humour and was reminded of it more often than I liked. This was mistake number two. I should have made my compost outside or in a bigger open shed.

However, the turned heap soon began to warm up again, steam at the top indicating hidden fires within (110° F. to 120° F.), and after three more turns at four-day intervals the bottling thermometer (which I had filched without my wife knowing it) registered 90° F. Spawning-time was approaching.

The manure was now a nice brown colour throughout, free of all lumpiness, having been well shaken out at each turning, damp but not wet, the straw breaking easily when twisted. Mistake number three. I had neglected to spray against manure flies during all the turnings.

Making the Bed.

The volume of the manure had now shrunk considerably as

a result of fermentation, so that I was able to lay out a good foot depth of compost covering the whole floor of the shed except for a space 4 ft. long and 3 ft. wide just inside the door. The whole of the compost-covered space was confined by a wall of loose bricks a foot high, and I had a handy 10-inch plank long enough to rest across the brick walls in any position so that I could pick the mushrooms (if any) without walking on the bed.

The compost was firmed gently into position with a fork and I was then all ready to spawn the bed when the internal temperature was steady at about 70° F. to 75° F.

Spawning.

I bought two cartons of spawn (bricks are now obsolete, a friable, dry cake being the order of the day), one from a well-known firm and the other from the window of our local ironmonger, and with my fingers (maker's instructions, and one can always wash after) pulled out a series of holes in the compost roughly an inch deep and 9 ins. apart, and into each hole I pressed a lump of the broken-up spawn, using pieces about as big as a walnut. With every hole so adorned I then covered the spawn over and firmed the bed once more. No mistakes occurred in this part of the proceedings.

Casing.

A week after spawning I dug up a few of the spawn-filled holes and sure enough a delicate white mould was spreading outwards from the spawn. The bed was now ready for casing.

Casing means covering the spawned bed with an inch or so of clean, weedless soil. I gathered that a rich loam was the best soil to use, and to avoid a bed of weeds one should use sterile soil. Soil taken from the second spit is considered sterile enough, so I dug the turfs off a section of the paddock and took out a few barrowloads of the soil beneath. One can assume that soil about 9 ins. below the top of the turf is weed free. Actually not one single weed appeared during the life of the bed.

This casing soil was carefully sifted clear of old tins, large bones, clinkers and decayed wire netting, in which our paddock is very rich, and a shovelful of hydrated lime was worked into each barrow-load. All was pretty well mixed, but the book said that the casing soil should have been got ready a week before, which, I suppose, was mistake number four.

It was now ten days after spawning, so I applied the inch coat of soil, carefully firming it down with a spade on to the springy compost, making a flat, smooth bed.

Cropping.

Now I had to sit back and wait for the crop, which was due to begin from five to eight weeks after spawning. Incidentally I noticed that "spawning can be done at any time of the year except possibly April, May and June, on account of increased fly trouble, but some growers now ignore this," etc. I decided that I was one of those who ignore. So far my programme had been as follows:

Manure heap made	..	May 25.
1st turned	.. ..	June 1.
2nd turn	.. ..	,, 5.
3rd turn	.. ..	,, 9.
4th turn	.. ..	,, 13.
Compost spawned	..	,, 18.
Cased ..	.. ..	,, 28.

On the fateful day of August 25th, after a week of hectic bombardment by the infernal buzz-bombs which roared overhead to explode in the distance or unpleasantly near, I had given up all hope of a crop, but that evening, wandering into the shed with a flash lamp, I was delighted to see clusters of tiny, white buttons peeping out of the casing soil all over the bed. A sizeable patch of some unknown toadstool had made an appearance some days before, but I was not to be taken in twice. Visions of luscious mushrooms on toast eked out with an odd rasher or even an occasional egg inflamed my imagination and coloured my buzz-bombed dreams as I slept in my dug-out beneath the beech tree.

By the morning of the 26th several of the buttons had grown a little. On the 27th I picked a handful but the little ones had in many cases gone brown, and pulling a few up I found them mere husks riddled with the tiny tunnellings which all pickers of field mushrooms know so well. Mistake number five: I had underestimated the fly peril.

Troubles.

I had not followed the instructions, and now began the most frenzied and not altogether unsuccessful blitz ever undertaken against the pests of the mushroom. As a fruit-grower of an experimental turn of mind I always keep a stock of enough poisons of one sort and another to destroy a whole village.

For a start I thought I would give a dose of two ounces of salt and an ounce of nicotine in a gallon of warmish water, applied with the watering can. I did so, and the next day there were a few sound mushrooms of edible size and a vast array of wormy buttons. I pulled up as many of the duds as I could, picked all the edibles, and gave the whole shed and everything within it a good spraying with Atomised Flit, which contains a good deal of pyrethrum. Also I rang up a friend who was trying out D.D.T., the new and potent fly insecticide, and begged a morsel. This material is said to be so powerful that one ounce properly applied will render 3,000,000,000 sq. ft. of surface toxic to flies. At first it seemed lacking in toxicity. There is little doubt, however, that dusting powders containing D.D.T. will fill a very useful place in the post-war mushroom grower's arsenal of anti-pest weapons.

Slugs appeared and ate large chunks out of the now improving crop of mushrooms. Metafuel and bran accounted for them. Woodlice established a few colonies among the loose bricks. This seems to be mistake number six. These vermin should not be encouraged by providing warm dry shelter. No other pests appeared to worry my mushrooms, and fortunately the various moulds which may afflict this crop kept away.

The mushrooms came in several flushes, and though I never quite controlled the fly there were times when the stalks were wholly innocent of borings; and the stalk is the point of first attack, so that a fairly clear stalk means a quite clear top. In addition to overeating and selling a nice surplus of mushrooms I used to fill wire trays with stalked and peeled specimens to dry in the gas oven.

Drying Mushrooms.

I found that drying mushrooms, especially those not fully expanded, took a shocking lot of gas, but filled the whole house with a most delicious aroma of cooking mushrooms for hours on end.

The result of the drying was to transform a three-inch mushroom into a little one-inch dried-up travesty as hard as wood. Some 30 lb. were so desiccated and stored in screw-topped bottling jars.

This method of drying is probably wrong and uneconomic. A mushroom has a very large water content, and a dark and savoury juice used to drip down and sully the clean enamel of the tray within the gas stove. This did not matter much, as during the buzz-bomb season I had evacuated my family to avoid showing them how terrified I was of those earth-shaking, explosive abominations of the perverted Adolf. So a little extra mess did not matter a great deal, and through the late summer I made jam and bottled fruit and dried mush-rooms wearing a tin hat and ready at a moment's notice to take cover in the dug-out. No casualties occurred, however, and nothing was wasted.

Years ago we had an Austrian cook, doubtless a spy, who dried the field mushrooms for winter use having first cut them into thin slices. In her case the drying was done in the Aga oven, so that no fuel was wasted, the heat being there for the taking.

To revive the whole dried mushroom in winter a few should be put into a dish and a little boiling water poured over them. There they can be left for twenty-four hours to soak, sliced up and used in soup and sauces, and jolly good they are too. The water which becomes dark brown has absorbed much of the flavour and should be used as the base for a soup just in the same way as the wise cook saves the water from boiled brussels sprouts and cabbage.

———

Now I have told you how greatly I underestimated the difficulties of mushroom growing, and if you decide to under-take it on even a small scale I would suggest that you buy a copy of the *Bulletin on Mushroom Growing*, published by H.M. Stationery Office, York House, Kingsway, London, W.C. 2. Follow the instructions exactly and you will not go far wrong. If (as I did) you find that the Bulletin is out of print, you may be able to obtain from Messrs. Geo. Monro, Ltd., of Waltham Cross, Herts., a copy of *The Culture of Mushrooms*, published by them at 2/6. As this firm are makers of mushroom spawn for commercial growers you may be sure that their instructions are entirely up-to-date. Failing even this source of information you will find a fairly full set of instructions in every carton of mushroom spawn which you buy.

There is also an excellent, practical and enticingly illustrated book called *Mushrooms and How to Grow Them*, written and published by John F. Barter, who in 1912 evidently grew mushrooms on a big scale at Napier Road, Wembley, Middlesex. I can find no trace of his whereabouts to-day, and am told that the firm ceased to exist some years back. If you come across his book, published at 1/-, it is worth having, though it does not contain all the modern technique for the control of insect and fungus pests.

It always annoys me to see mushrooms in the shops at 12/- and upwards a pound, but now that I have produced them for myself in more bulk than I could conveniently consume I shall never again look longingly at them in the shop window, considering whether or no to buy a quarter of a pound. Certainly not. I shall wait till my own crop comes along and have them fresh, pink-gilled and altogether delicious and for less than a quarter of the shop price.

Mushrooms on Lawns and in Pasture.

If you can do so, choose soil which is a good medium loam beneath the grass. Compost your manure as for indoor culture. Cut out a square foot of turf and dig out about 4 ins. or 5 ins. of soil. Fill the hole with the compost and place the spawn in the centre. Replace the turf and firm down. If you do this between May and the end of July you may pick mushrooms in August and September. Heavy rain after spawning may spoil your chance of a crop, and it is in any case unwise to go to much expense until a trial has shown the land to be satisfactory.

G

XVIII

THE WHYS AND WHEREFORES OF SPRING
FROSTS

ALTHOUGH, in peace-time, we import far more fruit than we grow, our home-produced total is by no means a negligible one, but it was not until after the disastrous frost of May, 1935 that the general public began to realise that the loss of up to four-fifths of the home fruit supply could not easily be replaced from abroad. Amateur fruit growers were especially hard hit, and that autumn many a jam cupboard was empty. When the catastrophe was repeated in 1938 heads were shaken and whispers were heard suggesting that a cycle of ice ages was imminent. However, the immense crop of 1939 lulled the anxieties of most of us, and, in any case, war was a far more exciting matter than the weather. In May, 1941, another frost devastated the fruit lands, and, though less severe and wide-spread than the previous visitations, the national fruit crop was reduced by a full half. By then shipping space was restricted and imports of fruit were but a drop in the ocean of demand. Frosts had become a matter of great importance to the individual and with three frosty years out of seven the subject deserves a little explanation.

Why Spring Frost Happens.

Sir Napier Shaw, a very eminent meteorologist, a good many years ago formulated the theory that each year between March and the end of May some three and a quarter billion tons of atmosphere must be transferred from the Northern Hemisphere to the Southern. Whether the passage is gradual or irregular is decided by the trend of those anti-cyclones, which, during the spring, bring high barometric readings, fog and fine weather, or occasionally, clear nights after chilly overcast periods.

During winter, and almost into early summer, our part of the earth loses more heat at night than it gains during the day. Sunshine in April and May warms us, but its effect is lost at night. In exactly the same way that the flaming mass of the sun radiates heat in all directions so the earth, deprived of solar warmth by night's shadow, radiates out her very small contribution of heat into the frightful cold of outer space until such time as the sun again appears. It is radiation loss at its full intensity which provides us with devastating spring frosts.

Conditions Favourable to Its Development.

In spring, when cold weather persists, with a high barometric pressure and overcast days, the advent of a still, starry night is likely to bring a frost. The risk is increased when the wind during previous days has veered to the north-west or north, following a spell of wet weather with westerly winds. Under such condition the air becomes drier, the wind drops, the sky clears and a frost is almost unavoidable.

How Frost Begins.

Dew Point, that degree of temperature at which summer air on a clear evening must discard some of its moisture content, is matched during winter and spring by hoar frost, when the night air, growing colder and colder, gives up part of its moisture at a temperature below freezing point, so that we see it as hoar frost on grass, leaves and roof-tops. This cooling down during the hours of darkness is the result of loss of heat by radiation. Every object exposed to the sky on a clear night must lose heat by radiation. The flow of heat rays is unseen but continuous, and the degree of cold reached by the surface of the object is decided mainly by the ability of the air surrounding it to counteract that loss by its own warmth.

This may sound a little complicated, but if you will picture a single leaf at the top of a tree 50 ft. high, radiating out its very modest contribution of comparative warmth in the chill of a spring night, you will appreciate that the leaf can become very little colder than the air which surrounds it. Leaves do stand at a slightly lower temperature than the surrounding air because they contain moisture which cools them by evaporation. If the air at our tree-top stands at a temperature, which during the night falls no lower than 35° F., the leaf surface is unlikely to drop below or even to freezing point, but at even a few degrees below air temperature its chilling effect on the air immediately in contact with it will begin a minute trickle of chilled air which will gravitate down to earth to join and collect with all the other minute trickles from

other leaves and will, eventually, constitute part of an appreciable amount.   As this layer of cold air deepens, the radiation
loss from exposed surfaces which are submerged beneath it
increases, for the neutralising effect of contact with warmer
air is lost.   Soon, since cold air, owing to increased density, is
appreciably heavier than an equal bulk of air a few degrees
less cold, the chilled air becomes deep enough for gravity to
impel it to motion and the drift to lower levels begins.

How a Spring Frost Develops.

Now from the high land and the hillsides a constant feed
of cold air comes to swell the pools already collecting in the
lower levels.   Descending as a very shallow film from the
slopes of the steeper hills its progress is slowed as less steep
ground is reached, the flow deepening as it progresses.   Further
collection of chilled air may have to take place on these easier
levels before a sufficient volume and weight of the heavier
cold air can get under weigh again.   Always the urge of this
icy drift is to fill up existing hollows first, to overflow them
and pass on to the lowest possible level where it can collect
and pool.

How deeply that ultimate level may become submerged in
frost-laden air is determined (a) by the amount of chilled air
which is produced during the night, i.e. the severity of the
frost, (b) by the preponderance of higher ground, or feed area,
to low ground or accommodation area and (c) the possibility,
or otherwise, of ultimate drainage to wide open spaces or to
sea level, which is the lowest level it is likely to find.

How Site Affects Your Fruit Trees.

If you have a garden on a hillock 50 ft. high, set in the
midst of an open plain with no higher land nearby, it is
extremely unlikely that any spring frost, save one of
phenomenal severity, will spoil your fruit blossom.   Cold
winds may prevent pollenising by insects, and gales may check
tree growth, but frost will not bother you.   This is because
the small amount of cold air draining from your particular
hillock will not be enough to raise the level of the frosty air
on the plain below, a level which in the most severe spring
frosts is unlikely to rise more than 30 ft. above soil level.

The frosts of mid-April 1938 left behind them on the level
ground between Peterborough and Wisbech a tide mark of

frost-damaged leaf and flower which showed that before the morning sun appeared to warm things up, chilled air had built up, or accumulated, on level ground, to a depth of about 10 ft. Had your hillock been on that Cambridgeshire flat you would have missed that damaging degree of frost and from within ten feet of the bottom up to the 50-ft. summit all damage would have been on a rapidly diminishing scale.

In frost records kept over a number of years on orchard land which rises from 300 ft. to 500 ft., the minimum temperature recorded at the top and at the half-way level can be as much as 14° warmer than the lowest levels. This means that while the crop in the low land may be practically wiped out by frost the fruit crop at the top will be undamaged.

Complications.

The hillock on the plain is a simple example. A saucer-like depression on a plain is equally simple, for just as the hillock escapes frost by discarding its chilled air, so a depression invites frost by offering ideal conditions for collection. There are in England large areas of mainly high land, such as the Cotswolds, and counties such as Suffolk, which is without a considerable hill but whose surface is undulating, or Sussex, where high hills and valleys lie behind the great barrier of the South Downs. All these are replete with frosty and frost-free areas, and the differentiation between liability to or freedom from damage in spring can be determined by the application of the formula mentioned earlier under the heads of (a), (b) and (c).

Because your garden stands at 300 ft. above sea level it is unsafe to pronounce it "frost-free." A high position associated with land contours which will shed cold air is excellent as a frost preventive, but height which still allows cold air from higher levels to collect upon it, or with contours around it which may guide currents of accumulated cold air draining from such higher land so that they pass over it, is very far from safe. Height in itself is no safeguard though relative height is the main essential for a frost-free site.

One should take a bird's-eye view, visualising the whole country under the stars of night as sweating out chilled air until the sweat begins to run down the hillsides to join the accumulation in the valleys and hollows. The natural watersheds of our rivers are potential sources of supply for chilled air. The river valleys are the collecting areas. The lowest levels are the most generally afflicted by frost, but whether that affliction will spread out as a shallow sea, or deepen to great depth and back up the valleys, will depend upon the land contours of the particular area concerned.   In a wide, shallow valley such as the Test valley above Romsey in Hants, frost level may be no higher than 20 ft. from river level.   In a deep land-locked valley with innumerable feeds from very high surrounding hills, such as the Wye valley at Ross-on-Wye, a bad spring frost will deepen to over a hundred feet and extremely low temperatures will be experienced.   On Ide Hill, overlooking the Kentish weald, spring and autumn frosts trouble the high gardens not at all, while the weald below lies deep in fog and biting cold.

Near to the sea, and by open estuaries, so large an area is often available for the moving flow of chilled air to spread and become shallow that frosts are serious only where the drainage flow is blocked by houses and belts of trees.   Sea and wide rivers reduce frost risk to the land adjoining them for the water itself stands at well above freezing point and loses so little heat that the chilled air flowing on to it from the land meets no cold air but is itself warmed by contact and can scarcely begin to accumulate.   So, while the deep and sheltered valley may be drowned in freezing air, the open flats beside the sea may be several degrees above freezing point.

From such examples it is possible to visualise and estimate one's frost risks.   It is easier to do this on the high land than on the intermediate levels between high and low where icy currents of air, often of some width and depth, pass slowly on to the lowest levels.   The mark of their passage can be traced by the blackened buds and shoots of oak and ash and walnut.   Where one tree is frosted and a neighbour is missed, the escape can usually be related to some dip, or fold, or tilt of the land which sets the air current off on a new tangent in its slow and serpentine course.

Fruit in the Garden.   The Danger Period.

Danger periods vary, since seasons may vary by a full month in leaf and blossom-bud development.   In 1935 most of the fruit was set when frost came on the night of May 16.   In 1938 the season was early and damage was done to bud and blossom by a series of late April frosts.   In 1941 the season was comparatively late, but the frost of May 15–16 caused much loss of blossom and bud.   1944 and 1945 were both frosty years.

In a frost of moderate severity (say down to 27° F.) the unopened bud suffers far less than the opening blossom. The fully open flower is more susceptible to fatal damage than the set and growing fruitlet. The period of liability to damage to fruit crops must begin in a normal season in mid-March when cherry-plum blossom is out and peaches are in bloom. It extends through April when plum, cherry, gooseberries and currants are in bloom, into May when pears are going out of flower and apples are well in flower. The end of the month will see the strawberries going out of blossom, so our danger period is roughly two months.

The thermometer on the garden wall, even if the mercury column is unbroken and not hopelessly involved with the tiny metal indicator within the tube, is little guide to the degree of cold which the individual blossom has to face. The gooseberry flower looking modestly downwards is shadowed by leaf and is far better protected than the more exposed flowers of the black currant, which faces outwards. The strawberry blossom within a few inches of the soil is worse off than either. On a radiation frost night all these blossoms, and the leaves belonging to them, are doing their part in manufacturing chilled air which will ultimately develop into a frost. In order that a frost shall arrive the air must be chilled by contact with their surfaces, which stand at a temperature lower than that of the air. As the level of chilled air deepens their radiation loss becomes more effective and at a few inches from the soil temperature may be 8°, or 10°, or more degrees colder than a few feet above the soil.

So our thermometer on the wall shows merely the approximate air temperature at its particular height above the ground which is quite unrelated with our strawberry blossom. The strawberry flower facing the open sky is subject to full radiation loss in all directions. The thermometer is shielded from much radiation loss since it does not face the sky and since a wall can retain a deal of heat, though the rime of frost along the wall top (there is none on the side) will serve to show what exposure to full radiation can extract from it.

Commercial fruit growers reckon that when a thermometer at 4 ft. from the ground in the open orchard shows 26° F. after a frosty night, much damage will have been done to their top fruit but that a proportion will come through. Apples, pears and plums have varietal reactions, for example, the Worcester Pearmain, with a light, long-stalked blossom will stand far more frost than a Cox or a Bramley, while a Czar, or a Burbank's Giant Prune, will come through a frost which will destroy the Victoria Plum crop.

Unless a thermographic record of night temperature variation is kept one has little idea of for how long a period the minimum temperature has lasted. The degree indicated on a recording thermometer may refer only to a matter of minutes, which will have been the peak low temperature for the early morning. The most damaging frosts are those which begin almost as soon as the sun has set and continue to deepen in intensity till morning. From the paragraph entitled "Complications," it will be realised that a garden may be in an area from which chilled air will drain away, but, unless the area which takes the air drainage is big enough to accommodate it, the rising level may eventually become high enough to submerge the garden and from a state of complete freedom from frost it will gradually become involved.

Preventing Frost Damage.

It is often easier to point a moral from personal experience than from generalisations. At times reports are needed on the liability or freedom from frost damage of a given site. In such cases the first thing to be looked for is to what extent shelter belts and dense hedges are likely to interfere with natural air drainage. If a well-situated orchard of fruit trees has a slight fall in one direction, and the outlet in that direction to lower levels is blocked by a hedge or shelter belt, the owner may be advised to remove a section so that air drainage can operate. Sometimes, nice, gentle slopes of well-ordered orchards are planted on both sides of a shallow valley, separated by a stretch of grass land and a meandering stream, along the banks of which rough bushes and big trees abound. The valley which would be a natural air-drainage duct, taking the chilled air from the two orchards, cannot serve its purpose until the trees and bushes are removed. On cold nights the sluggish flow of cold air will back up the valley sides and much fruit may be lost on the lower levels. Again even a 10-ft. high hedgerow at the lower end of a large, gently sloping field will cause serious loss of fruit, a loss which could easily be reduced by cutting the hedge down to a 5-ft. level in the case of top-fruit and removing it entirely if the orchard be of soft fruit.

Large-scale operations of this sort may seem to have little

bearing where garden practice is concerned, but there are many gardens where dense, high hedges at the lowest end prevent cold air from finding exit, and so cause damage to fruit. In such corners, even in frost-free years, the Morello cherries will suffer unduly from wilting blossom and dead wood as a result of Brown Rot, gooseberries will go down to Mildew, and strawberry leaves be unduly marked with the Leaf Spot, simply because shade and stagnant air allow the infective fungus spores to concentrate their attack instead of being dissipated in the natural movement of air.

While general assistance to certain gardens can be given by such methods, individual assistance to a patch of strawberries, a row of raspberries, or a peach or fig on a wall must be mechanical. One can cut out most of the actual temperature loss engendered by radiation by covering over the fruit one wishes to protect. For example, if one has a fruit cage the mere wire will do a little to reduce radiation loss, but if the top of the cage can be covered over with hessian on a frosty night, the loss from that patch will be almost entirely prevented, although the air temperature within the cage will approximate to air temperature in the open. Here the protection will amount to a rise of several degrees.

Any covering interposed between the object and the sky, be it a sheet of glass, a bit of muslin, a cloud in the sky or high cirrus cloud, will reduce radiation loss. Cloud in the sky at times nips a promising spring frost in the bud, if one may so reverse the simile, for cloud will reflect back heat rays being radiated from the earth level. Sometimes fog will do this. An Arizona grape-fruit grower stated that in the intensely dry atmosphere of that arid country radiation frosts were not unusual and could be damaging. His citrus groves were irrigated by artesian water standing at a temperature of 70° F., winter and summer, and all he had to do when frost threatened was to turn on the irrigation taps at the end of each row, when the warm water meeting the cold air set up a fog which blanketed his trees and cut out all risk of frost.

This is a blanket which one cannot easily duplicate; but try the effect of a sack laid over a gooseberry bush on a frosty spring night. Even a glass cloche, open at both ends, placed over a strawberry plant, will materially reduce the number of black-eyed blossoms which mean no fruit.

With such valuable crops as currants, raspberries and strawberries it should be well worth while, in private gardens, to plan cover against frosty nights. Acres of tobacco seedlings, and other young plants in the Far East, are so covered against sun in their early stages. Peaches in South Africa are protected against hail by overhead netting, but we suffer frost in our gardens with a philosophic complacency amounting to fatalism. The orchard heater pots, burning fuel oil, are not for the amateur; to be successful they must be used in bulk over several acres or the heat generated merely drifts off instead of warming the immediate surroundings. Nor is the smoke from a few bonfires of any avail, for in a spring frost there is no wind and their smoke rises vertically instead of drifting along the surface, while its value as a returning agent for radiation loss is far less than cloud.

The Germans before the war were advertising fog generators for use in market gardens, but as they used a very corrosive acid they are not likely to be popular here. Anericans were still playing—though less hopefully—with wind towers, whereon large air-propellers, operated by old aero-engines, forced a proportion of the warmer upper air downwards in a vain effort to mix the two and achieve an intermediate temperature. In California a patent had actually been filed for an anti-freeze mixture with which to spray one's trees. An admirable system, especially if it could be adapted to the outside of car radiators or used as a salve against chilblains! Now in 1947 growers in England are experimenting with tractor-drawn "frost-blowers." These are powerful fans which drive a sixty-mile-an-hour gale through the trees. The results are not yet available, since 1947 was a frost-free spring.

From this brief outline we can see that to be free of frost damage when our neighbours' gardens are devastated we must first of all choose our site carefully. To reduce frost liability in a less well-placed site, we must plan, as far as we may, for free air drainage, and in a badly placed site we must cover up as far as possible and hope for the best.

Forecasting Frost.

If you are anxious to know by early evening whether you may expect a frosty night, this can be forecast by using a combination of the wet bulb and dry bulb thermometers. The mercury in the wet bulb thermometer, being surrounded by a little wick of muslin dipping into water, will, when the air is dry, indicate a lower temperature than the wet bulb thermometer, owing to the increased coldness produced around its bulb by the evaporation of the water. By comparing the varying temperature of the two thermometers with a table supplied with the instrument some idea of the degree of severity of the night's frost can be ascertained. If, during the late afternoon of a clear day with no wind, the wet bulb temperature is well below the dry bulb, a frost can be expected early in the evening. If the difference is not noticeable until the evening the frost may be expected later on in the night, provided always that no breeze springs up and no clouds come upon the scene.

Americans are now using a different method which seems to answer well enough and needs only an ordinary thermometer. They reckon that in typical spring-frost weather, with calm clear nights, there is a uniform rate of fall in temperature from the afternoon maximum through the night until the morning minimum, and that the times for such maximum and minimum temperatures will be approximately the same for all such days. This means to say that if one knows the maximum temperature and takes a reading at mid-way between afternoon and next morning the minimum temperature will be in ratio.

If, therefore, the maximum temperature on any day at 3.30 p.m. is 70° F., and the minimum temperature at 5 a.m. the next morning is 30° F. and the median, or mid-way, temperature at 10.15 p.m. is 50° F., the difference between the median temperature and the maximum temperature (in this case 20°) if subtracted from the median temperature will indicate the expected minimum to be 30° F. Suppose, on the day following, the afternoon maximum is only 50° F., and the median is 32° F., the subtraction of median from maximum gives us 18°, and 18° from 32° F. means that a drop to 14°F. is to be expected, which is an extremely severe frost and one that we can very well do without. This system is simple enough for any one to test out and is worthy of a trial.

XIX

MANURING AND COMPOST HEAPS

For all practical purposes we may divide manures into two categories—organic and inorganic. The dictionary describes organic as "pertaining to plants or animals," and inorganic as "not having organic structure, as rocks, metals, etc." Both are poor definitions and very incomplete.

Farmyard manure and compost are both complete organic manures, and except that farmyard manure contains the waste products of digestive juices and a good deal of urine with all its valuable salts, an analysis of farmyard and an analysis of compost are very similar. Both are entirely of organic origin and both rot down to the type of humus which rejoices the hearts (if any) of the myriad beneficial bacteria which populate our soil and break down vegetable matter to energise our crops. If you look up humus in the dictionary you will find it as "soil or mould, especially of decayed vegetation." Actually it is a by-product of bacterial activity.

The inorganic fertilisers may be simple compounds such as sulphate of ammonia, the various forms of potash and treated phosphatic limestone, basic slag and so on. They contain essential plant foods but they contain no humus. Mixed, inorganic fertilisers, sold as complete plant foods at high prices, often contain added organic material to give bulk and texture, but generally speaking the inorganic are completely lacking in humus.

The organic manures, dung and compost, contain more humus than anything else, but they also contain nitrogen, phosphate and potash in small but very available proportions. Other organic manures such as hoof and horn meal, furrier's waste, rabbit flic and feathers contain nitrogen and little else of value. You will recall that when young ladies in Victorian days suffered from fainting fits as a result of over-tight lacing with consequent indigestion, a burning feather was held under the nose to revive them. The nitrogen freed from the burning feather being mainly in the form of ammonia took the place of the bottle of smelling salts which contain the inorganic form.

Dried blood, which sounds horrid, is often advocated as a vegetable manure to provide nitrogen in a very acceptable form over a considerable period. Nitrate of soda which gives inorganic nitrogen is extremely quick acting and for this reason is used where a rapid response is needed. Bone meal, especially in the raw state, provides nitrogen and phosphate in varying amounts, both being given up over a period of time which is determined by the fineness of the grinding.

For potash in the organic form, unless we can collect seaweed, we have to rely upon wood ashes or any bonfire ash resulting from the burning of vegetable waste. The shortage of inorganic potash makes it essential that all bonfire ash should be spread as soon as possible to avoid losing the valuable but soluble content.

Trace Elements in Manure.

A ton of well-made farmyard manure which has been protected from wind and rain may contain 12 lb. of nitrogen, 6 lb. of phosphoric acid (which means phosphates) and 12 lb. of potash. These amounts are, of course, appreciable quantities, but tucked away in that ton of manure will be traces of boron, calcium, iron, magnesium, manganese, sodium, silicon, zinc and half a dozen other elements which make up a very interesting little collection. They have all been drawn up from the soil and sub-soil by the plants which went to make up the manure, and as manure, they return to the soil once more.

These trace elements which are present in soluble form in most soils play an important part in building up a healthy plant or tree. While invariably found in animal manure and in compost made from rotted vegetation they do not occur in straight inorganic manures of the sulphate of ammonia, superphosphate and sulphate of potash types. It is almost impossible when feeding a soil with farmyard manure or compost to upset the balance of the trace elements in the soil, but it is extremely easy to do this by applying inorganic manures. Deficiency symptoms may then appear, and it is often difficult to remedy them. Deficiencies of such substances as iron, boron, potash and magnesium are soon indicated by various unhealthy symptoms which develop in the plant or tree.

Soil Bacteria.

While certain plants—clover, lucerne and lupins are a few —fix gaseous nitrogen by organisms which cause small swellings on the roots, nitrogen is also fixed by certain bacteria in the soil which are called Azotobacter. Their energy is dependent upon the amount of decaying vegetable matter or humus which is available in the soil. In an ounce of loam soil rich in humus there may be 150,000,000 of these bacteria, Azotobacter being only one of the group.[1] Ranged against the beneficient soil bacteria are various microscopic enemies, the most deadly being the protozoa, which in over-manured soil may prove a serious check to the activities of the former. Soil bacteria play a very important point in breaking down organic manures so that solutions of the various constituents of the manure can be absorbed by the hairs of the plant roots from the water in the soil. Everything a plant has to work with is dependent primarily on root action and must be in solution form.

Nutrient Solutions and Hydroponics.

It is, however, possible to take sterile sand free of all organic manures and humus and having made up a suitable solution of various chemicals to maintain the solution in circulation through the sand and so to feed and grow plants with chemicals and nothing else.

In Hydroponics or soilless culture the plants are anchored in some substance such as wood wool on a wire frame and drop their roots into a nutrient solution below. These are both specialised methods of culture which may almost be said to have proved that soil is unnecessary. It will, however, be noted that having replaced the anchorage provided by soil both these methods depend for their success upon unlimited supplies of water. No inorganic manures can give us that.

Humus or rotted vegetable matter in the soil holds up a great deal of water, quite apart from any beneficent bacterial activity, and we know that there are good and extremely evil bacteria contending for supremacy. Sterilised soil (heat or various chemicals will destroy all soil life) gives the good bacteria a useful start, but the evildoers soon creep in again, which is why the commercial tomato grower must sterilise his soil annually.

Few soils are ideal in structure. Some, as we know, resemble plasticine for much of the year, others set like concrete, and both these will be lightened and sweetened by humus. Other soils are sandy and soon dry out, their free air movement

---

[1] In *Microbes by the Million* (A Pelican Special), Dr. Nicol states that 2,000,000,000 bacteria are normally present in a saltspoonful of soil. The enquiring reader will find the bacterial side of composting dealt with in an interesting and understandable way in this volume.

makes them what the farmer calls "hungry," for they burn up manure rapidly. To the sandy soil humus will give cohesion and moisture-holding capacity. Loams are usually well up on humus content but are unlikely to be over-supplied. Peaty soils have a superabundance of humus in an acid and undigested form.

Having secured the right soil consistency you can please yourself whether you retain it by using natural organic manures or burn up your humus with inorganic manures from a tin. In either case it is well to remember that neither system can work to full effect without a solid backing and regular replacement of humus. Personally I prefer organic manures for every possible occasion but am prepared to admit that many soils are so ill-constituted for growing certain fruits and vegetables that to make horticulture economically possible one must add inorganic potash, organic or inorganic phosphate and an occasional cocktail of a nitrogenous fertiliser, whether it be from the gas works as Sulphate of Ammonia or extracted under colossal pressures from the air we breathe and fixed as Nitro Chalk.

Compost versus Artificial Manuring.

There are market gardeners who swear by compost or farmyard manure and use little else. One grower of my acquaintance, who has sixteen acres under glass, composts down every tomato stem and leaf and every bit of vegetable matter from cabbage leaves to his neighbour's grass and hedge trimmings that he can lay hands on, and affirms that there is nothing like humus for quality production (Plate XV). Others alternate organics with inorganics and are satisfied. Many fruit growers consistently apply Nitrogen, Phosphate and Potash from the bag, plough in a weed crop at the end of the season, and assure me that nothing else is necessary. One told me that he had done this for over thirty years and grew good and fairly regular crops. It may take a drought season to expose the fallacy of such a creed. It is, however, no secret that one of our largest and most successful market gardeners relies almost entirely upon compost and farmyard manure to produce crops which invariably top the market for quality and flavour.

I consider the manurial subject of so much importance that I have asked Sir Albert Howard, C.I.E.,* who initiated the Indore system of composting in India and who is, one can say, the Father of Humus, to reply to a few leading questions which

* All good gardeners deplored his death in 1947.

are typical of the inquiring amateur who would like to compost but has his doubts.   Here is what he says:

1. "*What is the smallest amount of compost I can expect to make properly?* This depends on local circumstances such as (1) the amount of vegetable waste which can be collected outside the garden in the form of fallen leaves, hedge and bank trimmings (June and October), roadside collections when the verges are tidied up in the autumn, seaweed and so forth; (2) the amount of vegetable waste from the lawns, borders and area under vegetables; and (3) the amount of dustbin and kitchen waste.

In running small heaps two difficulties have to be overcome on account of the small size of the heaps and the relatively large cooling surface (which, of course, decreases as the volume increases).   These are: (1) excessive rain, which often makes the heaps sodden and cuts off the air supply, and (2) the cooling effect of wind, frost and snow.

These difficulties can be got over by the use of the New Zealand box, or better still by two small bricked pits, flush with the ground with the bottom of earth (to promote aeration). These pits can be in a border with a small earthen platform a little bigger than one pit for maturing the compost after the second turn.   The procedure is as follows: one pit—the one away from the platform—is first filled with mixed wastes, manure and earth in the ordinary way and provided with an aeration vent in the middle.   At the time of the first turn this is forked into the second pit.   At the time of the second turn the material is stacked on the earth platform to ripen.   Composting is continuous throughout the year.   The pits put the wind out of action and a simple covering can be provided to keep off excessive rain.

In New Zealand the owners of small gardens use a frame or box for compost manufacture which makes the job both easy and tidy.   The box has neither top nor bottom, only four sides, one of which is detachable, fastened by thumbscrews. The sides measure about 4 ft. 6 ins. long and 3ft. high.   The boards which make the sides have $\frac{1}{2}$-in. gaps between them to allow for the entry of air.

The wastes, manure and earth are thrown in layer by layer, and the vertical holes are made by a crowbar as usual.

After a month the loose side is unscrewed and the box is drawn off the heap.   The box is then screwed up again, of course empty, and the heap is forked into it, beginning from the top, that is, it is turned and the vertical holes are remade. After a month it is turned again—that finishes all labour on it.

The New Zealand box acts quite well—composting takes place right up to the boards even in a hard winter like that of 1942.

2. *If I do make compost, can I expect it to do all my manuring or should I reinforce it with organic manures such as dried blood, bone meal and so forth?* Yes. None of these things are necessary as additions, but during the first year while experience is being obtained in making compost, they may be useful.

3. *If I use compost prepared on the Indore lines can I use inorganic manures such as sulphate of ammonia, superphosphate and sulphate of potash?* No. Inorganics are quite unnecessary, because compost when oxidised in the soil provides all the NPK (the manurial formula denoting Nitrogen, Phosphate and Potash) needed. This reaches the plant in two ways: (1) via the root hairs and (2) by the mycorrhizal association. The latter is a composite structure made up of threads of fungus tissue (mycelium) which feed on the soil humus and surround or invade the young cells of the root, where fungus and plant cell live together in partnership (symbiosis). Eventually the fungus threads, which are rich in protein, are digested, the products of digestion passing up to the leaves in the sap current. The roots of the trees and plants, therefore, feed in two ways simultaneously—by means of the salts absorbed by the root hairs and by means of the proteins and carbohydrates of the mycorrhizal association.

4. *Is it a fact that if my potatoes go down with blight I can put the haulms into the compost without risk of carrying on disease, and can I do the same with mouldy tomatoes and stems of diseased tomato plants?* Most emphatically, yes. The advice to the contrary is based on the fears of laboratory hermits, not on experience. The large glasshouse grower whom you mention, found that, when he took my advice to compost his diseased tomatoes and apply the compost to the same area to grow another crop of tomatoes.

5. *In the modern house with W.C. sanitation there will only be a small amount of urine available, but if this is daily thrown on a humus dump will it not be too strong? Can I add this and a regular amount of dry soil so as to absorb it or will too much soil spoil the humus?* No, but it must not be used in excess to make the heaps or pit sodden. Any excess can be poured

on earth to make "urine earth" which in turn can either go on the land direct or be used in composting. In this case an extra pit for making urine earth would be an advantage.

6. *Where the rottable waste is small in quantity can I expect to get enough heat to destroy weed seeds? Does this mean that I must get the weed cut and on the heap before seed heads are forming?* Yes, if pits or the New Zealand box are used, but in such cases the mixture of vegetable and animal waste must be an intimate one.

Of course with small heaps and generally speaking it is an advantage not to let the weeds seed. Their life histories ought to be cut short in the vegetative phase.

The Indore Method of Composting.

The following instructions for the making and management of the compost heap follow the method known as the Indore Process, which is described in detail in *An Agricultural Testament* and in the *Gardeners' Chronicle* of April 13th, 1940. The method has the merit that not only is it truly economical, in that "waste" materials are salvaged, but also that weed seeds and harmful insects and fungi are destroyed and vegetables grown with its use are disease-resisting and of unequalled food value.

Materials.

The first requirement is "organic wastes," that is plant residues: weeds, leaves, old straw and hay, bracken, reeds, seaweed, hedge trimmings, etc. Paper, worn-out clothing, leather and sacking can also be added after previous soaking in water. All green material should be withered. Hard woody material should be cut into short lengths and crushed where possible by, for example, wheel traffic. Anything very resistant (lignins or leather) can be transferred from heap to heap if the first is not enough to break it down.

The second requirement for the compost heap is animal manure, from horses, cattle, sheep, pigs, rabbits or poultry. Nothing is better than freshly used night soil for this purpose, which, if the composting be well done, is safe and entirely without offence.

The third requirement is earth, if possible with lime, as ground limestone or chalk, wood ash, or even finely riddled coal ash, or preferably a mixture of all. The earth, etc., is needed as a neutralising agent.

The fourth requirement is water.   In general rain will supply this need (in fact it may be said that protection from rain is more important in this country than the provision of water although there are occasions when it must be added).   The heap must not be too wet, the consistency of a squeezed sponge being aimed at.   Liquid manure (for instance, bedroom slops or drainage from a pig cote) is of the very highest value.

During the early stages of decomposition air is required in large quantities by the fungi and germs in the heap.   This is got by diffusion from the atmosphere, so the heap must be made loose.   Later, after the fungous stage is over and the material has crumbled and darkened, the heap has reached a stage where the fermentation goes on without air.   The germs obtain their oxygen from the decomposing material itself.

Making the Compost Heap.

1. *Composition of the Heap.*

Make square or oblong heaps upon earth, NOT concrete. If possible, a bottom should be made in a similar manner to that of a haystack.   Hedge trimmings, bush fruit prunings or other materials which will act as an open base are suitable. This assists aeration.   On this base the heap is built.   It consists of a horizontal layer of about 6 ins. of mixed organic wastes followed by a thin layer, about 2 ins., of animal manure, followed in its turn by a good sprinkling of earth containing, where these are available, wood ashes and lime, preferably in the form of chalk or ground limestone.   This three-layer sandwich, the wastes, the manure, the earth and ash is repeated until a height of from 4 ft. to 5 ft. is reached.   (It will sink later).   The final layer of manure should be about twice the previous thickness and the final sprinkling of earth should completely cover the manure.

In districts of heavy rainfall it is advisable to arrange for the finishing layers to form a double slope.

In most districts of England a temporary covering is ESSENTIAL to protect the heap against excessive rain. Boughs or poles should be laid across the heap to raise the covering.

2. *Size of the Heap.*

The minimum size for a heap is 5 ft. by 5 ft. by 4 ft. high. With any side smaller the ratio of cooling surface to volume is too great.   When making small heaps it is better to build the second up against the first and so on. The heat is then conserved. It can be planned so that the turnings, referred to later, follow each other and the benefits of a larger heap are thus maintained.

Space must be allowed for turning the heap. Two turns are required to complete the process.

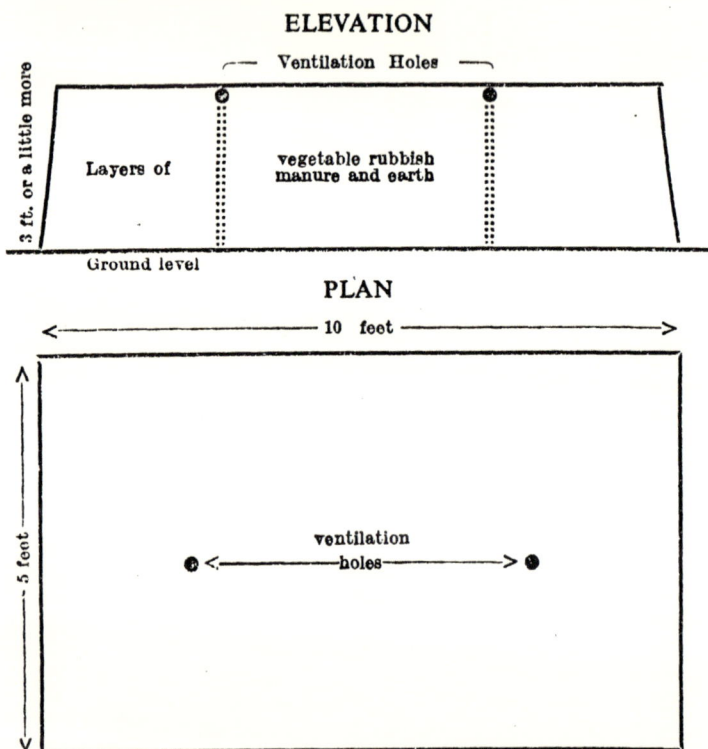

ELEVATION

┌── Ventilation Holes ──┐

3 ft. or a little more

Layers of   vegetable rubbish
                 manure and earth

Ground level

PLAN

←────── 10 feet ──────→

5 feet

ventilation
● ←──────holes──────→ ●

3. *Supply of Air.*

It is very important that the heap should be made as loose as possible in order to permit of copious aeration, and care should be taken not to step on the heap whilst building.

It has been found that in this country aeration can be greatly assisted by making in the heap vertical holes by means of a rod or crowbar. Some people stand a rod upright first and make

the heap around it.   The holes can be made 4 ins. or 6 ins.
wide by pushing the rod to and fro.   The holes should be 3 ft.
apart.

4. First Turn.

An intense fermentation sets in during three weeks and the
temperature of the heap rises to about 150° F.   The material
inside the heap turns white owing to the development of
fungous growth.

At the end of three or four weeks the heap is turned from
one end to a new site, care being taken to bring the outside
to the inside of the re-made heap.   Holes should again be
bored in the turned heap.

When turning for the first time, vertical slices should be cut,
after the manner of cutting bread, of about 9 ins. to 1 ft.
by means of a fork.

5. Second Turn.

The temperature, which will fall towards the end of the first
three weeks, again rises.   Within ten days of the first turn the
material starts to crumble and darken.   *Bacteria* now take a
leading share in the process.

About two months after the heap was originally made it is
turned a second time; again the outside is brought to the
inside and, where necessary, protection from rain is given.
No holes are required after the second turn.   A spade should
be used to cut the heap at the second turn, the slices being
about 6 ins. wide.

6. Completion, Position of Heap, and General Management.

Three months after the process began the material is ready
for application to the land.   It consists of a finely divided
product of which about 80 per cent will pass through a sieve
of six meshes to the inch.

Protection against excessive rain has already been mentioned.
The opposite possibility of dryness must be watched for and if
rain be insufficient, water must be added.   This must not be
sluiced on to the heap with a bucket but sprayed either by a
hose with a nozzle or from a can with a rose.   If water be
added at the time of turning this rule does not hold and water
from a bucket may be sprinkled on to the material cut from
the heap before it is re-made into the new heap.   This method

should, however, be used WITH DISCRETION and the material thoroughly mixed before it is added to the re-made heap in order to distribute the moisture. It has already been mentioned that the material should have sufficient moisture to give it the consistency of a squeezed sponge. That is the guide to which the maker should work. It is impossible to lay down a hard and fast rule concerning either the protection of the heap from rain or the addition of water in the absence of rain. The heap has life and must be looked after like all living things.

If a sheltered site can be chosen facing south and with a wind-break from the north, so much the better. This applies particularly where the heaps are only 5 ft. or 6 ft. square, and for these smaller heaps, where possible, protection should be given on three sides by means of walls or hedges; but the heap must never be banked up against a wall. The system by which mutual protection is given by old and new heaps should also be used wherever possible.

So much for Sir Albert Howard's system of manuring without artificials, which, however, demands the intermixing of animal manure with the plant wastes. Many people cannot get the farmyard manure to make humus in the ideal form, but when weeds, nettles, green hedge trimmings, cabbage leaves and such rottable waste can be had it is simple enough to build up a heap using these wastes, and occasionally sprinkling the level top of the heap with burnt earth from the bonfire. Such a heap, if raised to fair dimensions, will in time rot down even without turning and provide usable humus, with the one great advantage over inorganic manures that it cannot spoil soil texture or balance.

Various "accelerators" to speed up compost making are available to-day and provided they come from reputable firms can be relied up to do what is promised.

INDEX

Printed in the United Kingdom by
Lightning Source UK Ltd., Milton Keynes
141068UK00001B/143/A

9 781406 793543